Network Marketing: Learn How to Creating Your Network Marketing Business, Find out the 7 Habits of Highly Effective Network Marketer Professionals
By: Florino Alfeche

TABLE OF CONTENTS

- **Chapter 1**
- Making Plans for your Network Marketing Business
- Recruiting MLM Distributors Effectively
- Identifying the Types of Distributors
- Distributors' Network Marketing Strategies
- Developing a Distribution Channel Strategy
- Starting Your Own Network Marketing Business
- Organizational and Management Setup
- How to Advertise and Market Your Business
- **Chapter 2**
- The 7 Commandments
- Of Network Marketing Leaderships
- **Chapter 3**
- Choosing your Network Marketing Business
- **Chapter 4**
- How to Research a Business Opportunity
- Types of Business Opportunities
- How Government Protects You
- Franchises vs. Business Opportunities
- The Advantages of a Business Opportunity
- The Disadvantages of a Business Opportunity
- Guidelines for Choosing a Business Opportunity
- Evaluating a Potential Opportunity
- What the Disclosure Statement Tells You
- Analyzing the Financial Statements
- **Chapter 5**
- Remember that it is a Business
- Understanding the Universal Laws of Business
- Network Marketing is a Numbers Game
- Manage your Time, and Profitability

- ❖ **Chapter 6**
- ❖ Start Your Network Marketing Business Today
- ❖ The Top Three Principles to Build a Successful MLM Business
- ❖ More Profitable in Your Network Marketing Business
- ❖ **Chapter 7**
- ❖ Winning Strategy for Your Network Marketing Business
- ❖ Most Critical Skill Every Network Marketer Professional Must Possess
- ❖ **Chapter 8**
- ❖ The Building Real Residual Income to your
- ❖ Network Marketing Business
- ❖ **Chapter 9**
- ❖ Overcoming Challenges, Obstacles, and Fear
- ❖ TRUE SELF VERSUS FALSE SELF
- ❖ **Chapter 10**
- ❖ Raise Your Self Esteem for Success in Network Marketing
- ❖ CREATE AN ACTION PLAN CONSISTENT WITH YOUR VISION
- ❖ AFFIRM YOUR STRENGTHS AND ACKNOWLEDGE YOURSELF DAILY
- ❖ Conclusion

© Copyright 2017 by Florino Alfeche - All rights reserved.

This document is geared towards providing exact and reliable information in regards to the topic and issue covered. The publication is sold with the idea that the publisher is not required to render accounting, officially permitted, or otherwise, qualified services. If advice is necessary, legal or professional, a practiced individual in the profession should be ordered.

- From a Declaration of Principles which was accepted and approved equally by a Committee of the American Bar Association and a Committee of Publishers and Associations.

In no way is it legal to reproduce, duplicate, or transmit any part of this document in either electronic means or in printed format. Recording of this publication is strictly prohibited and any storage of this document is not allowed unless with written permission from the publisher. All rights reserved.

The information provided herein is stated to be truthful and consistent, in that any liability, in terms of inattention or otherwise, by any usage or abuse of any policies, processes, or directions contained within is the solitary and utter responsibility of the recipient reader. Under no circumstances will any legal responsibility or blame be held against the publisher for any reparation, damages, or monetary loss due to the information herein, either directly or indirectly.

Respective authors own all copyrights not held by the publisher.

The information herein is offered for informational purposes solely, and is universal as so. The presentation of the information is without contract or any type of guarantee assurance.

The trademarks that are used are without any consent, and the publication of the trademark is without permission or backing by the trademark owner. All trademarks and brands within this book are for clarifying purposes only and are the owned by the owners themselves, not affiliated with this document.

Introduction

In this course, Florino Alfeche who is known as the best-selling author in money making will show you how to prepare for a transition to networking marketing. Begin by taking a look at your career goals, the systems that will support you, and proper ways to plan for success. Find out how to marshal your resources, refine your portfolio for presentation to clients, and estimate your costs to avoid any surprises on the financial front. Plus, discover how to create invoices, manage your books and taxes, expand your client base with marketing, and grow your business.

He will emphasize how essential people are to your networking marketing career. They give you guidance, expand your capabilities, and help you get clients; but your professional network does have its limits, especially if you're moving into an unfamiliar area. This book also talks about how to reach an audience if you don't already have contacts within it. You'll have to get inside this new group, first by identifying it and then by gaining allies there.

Here are three ways to do this: The first has the lowest barrier to entry. Get to know the unfamiliar field as well as you can through online research. Find out who is important in it, where its practitioner's hangout, what is important to them and the terms they use to describe themselves. You need to know both the subject and the culture surrounding it to get your foot in the door. Then find and read active online discussions in that community and contribute when you feel ready. Relationships naturally form this way, as you get to know them and they get to know you. The second method is to research the new field, then approach someone for what is called an informational interview. Make it as the low commitment as possible and make it absolutely clear that you're looking only for advice, not a job.

It may sound unlikely but thinks of it. If you got an email from someone nicely asking you for a little advice in your area of expertise, wouldn't you provide it? And if they were local and offered to buy you lunch, wouldn't you take it? The third method is to research the area then get to know the people involved through real-world group meetings. These trade shows are great for this because the mix of exhibitors tells you exactly what's important in a given area. But user groups, trade association meetings, parties, and lunches are all good as well.

You're not there to sell. Rather you're there to figure out who wants to buy what you're offering or how to change it, so they will. So, you found your new audience, how do you reach them?

Here are a few ways: If all is gone well with your research and interactions, you'll have gained new contacts and the field is no longer outside your professional network, so you can just market your services as usual. But if you haven't gained that foothold, you'll want to use online methods to drive this new audience to your website.

Chapter 1
Making Plans for your Network Marketing Business

If you are thinking about starting a business out of your home in your spare time, multilevel marketing, often called MLM, may be a good choice for you. A multilevel marketing company provides products and resources to its distributors, so when you become a distributor, your job is to attract other people to become distributors, supervised by you. When they produce revenues by selling the products to customers and building their own networks of distributors, you get a cut. The key to success in multilevel marketing is your ability to attract people to buy your products or join your distribution network.

Make a List
Start your marketing plan by making a list of people you know. You are looking for two categories of people: potential distributors and potential customers. Some network marketing companies allow you to place products in existing retail stores or flea market booths, but other MLM companies restrict distributorships to individuals only. Verify the policies of your MLM with regards to who may become a distributor. Developing a distributor at a level below you -- or "downline" -- and customers is a numbers game: The more people you pitch, the greater your chances of success. Be prepared to pitch as many as 100 people before you find one enthusiastic distributor or customer. Even one distributor in your downline exponentially increases your likelihood of adding more distributors and customers.

Plan Your Pitch
Most MLM companies provide a script to use in pitching products and distributorships when you first start out. As you become familiar with this script you can customize it to your own style and the buying behavior of your contact list. In making your marketing plan, define the demographics of your contact list in terms of their personal buying habits, whether they can best be reached online or via traditional advertising, the approximate size of their network of friends and associates, and what element of the MLM enterprise would be most appealing. Current MLM distributors are often interested in representing additional products, so perfect your pitch and contact them first.

Plan Events
One way to maximize the number of people you can pitch is to hold informational events. These can take the form of parties at your home or more formal meeting presentations held in public venues such as hotels, church meeting rooms, and civic clubs. One benefit of using meeting space at churches and civic clubs is the potential that they might consider distributing your products as a fundraising project. In planning your marketing, look for advantageous tie-ins such as this.

Promote
The next step in your marketing plan is to figure out how to spread the word. Word-of-mouth marketing is an effective way to attract people to your pitch events. This is done by inviting your list to your events and

encouraging each person to bring a friend. If your MLM provides distributor websites, promote your events by aggressively announcing them on social media sites and online advertising sites, directing people to your distributor website for information. In most cases, once they sign into your distributor website, they automatically become your lead, and, even if they contact your MLM Company directly, you will receive credit and they will be placed in your downline. Check your MLM's policies on these types of referrals.

Recruiting MLM Distributors Effectively

Multilevel marketing companies offer independent contractors the ability to earn substantial revenue from building a distribution network. These networks include every distributor they directly recruited as well as the people those distributors recruit. Rather than earning a fee for recruiting new distributors, MLM distributors can earn small commissions from sales made by distributors below them in the network, called downline distributors. The true income potential of an MLM distributor comes from building a large downline network.

Identifying the Types of Distributors

People become MLM distributors for different reasons, looking to accomplish different objectives. Some are enthusiastic customers who become a distributor to earn a commission on their own purchases, while others are opportunity seekers excited about the business opportunity. Still, others are veteran distributors who are open to more lucrative opportunities. The two ways a distributor benefits from his recruits is from their sales, and their recruits' sales. An impressive sized network of distributors is worthless if the only activity new recruits do is recruiting new distributors.

Know Your Target

Successfully recruiting new distributors requires approaching people capable of signing up in a situation favorable to the sales pitch. The sales pitch must address their needs and objectives. For example, a distributor notices that one of his customer's orders enough that her commission as a distributor would exceed the franchising cost of becoming a distributor. He could point out to this customer that, by signing up as a distributor, she could effectively receive a discount that would save her money on her current purchases. Similarly, an opportunity seeker must first be sold on the income potential of the MLM model, whereas an experienced MLM distributor just needs to know whether a new company could provide a better payout.

Qualify Leads
Finding new leads to work is vital to any business, and recruiting MLM distributors is no different. Many successful network builders qualify leads for new distributors as they make their product sales pitches. Briefly mentioning the business opportunity after closing every sale allows distributors to identify interested leads. They can then follow up through informational sessions where they can pitch the opportunity in more detail. Networking at meetings for direct sales professionals introduces distributors to other experienced MLM distributors.

Provide Support
Failure rates for MLM distributors are astronomically high. More than 99 percent of people who sign up with an MLM company will never earn a profit. Distributors often succeed or fail based on the support and training they receive from their recruiter. Developing a reputation as a supportive recruiter with a number of successful recruits attracts opportunity seekers and experienced distributors when deciding what MLM company is best for them.

Distributors' Network Marketing Strategies
Distributors provide sales and marketing service that enables other companies to sell to customers they could not reach with their own resources. Distributors can act on behalf of a number of companies or operate as franchised outlets for a single company. Depending on their relationship with each company, distributors may develop their own marketing strategy or operate a cooperative strategy with their channel partners.

Priorities
Distributors' marketing strategies operate at two levels. They aim to increase their own customer base so that they can grow revenue and improve opportunities to win additional distribution agreements. They also aim to sell more of each channel partner's products so they can attract more cooperative marketing funds or increased levels of marketing support. When developing their strategy, distributors may give

preference to channel partners that offer better levels of support or products with higher margins.

Customer Base

Distributors develop strategies to increase the numbers of customers and prospects for the different products they distribute. In some cases, they target smaller prospects while the channel partner deals directly with larger customers. If a partner is using distributors to increase geographical reach, the distributor may target both small and large prospects. Distributors find new prospects in a number of ways. They may register their details on a partner's database of local distributors, relying on the partner to drive business by recommending authorized distributors. Alternatively, they may generate sales leads and inquiries by running advertising or direct marketing campaigns using their own budgets or cooperative marketing funds.

Sales

Distributors deal with customers through a direct sales team. As part of their strategy to improve sales, distributors take advantage of their partners' sales and product training programs to improve the performance of the sales team. Distributors structure their sales teams to either cover geographical territories or focus on specific market sectors or product categories. They set sales targets that will enable them to maximize rebates and support from channel partners.

Branding

Branding is an important element of distributor marketing strategy. By adopting the branding of a channel partner, a distributor can benefit from recognition and brand awareness the partner has created through its own marketing programs. This can make it easier for distributors to gain acceptance in the market when approaching new prospects. Distributors that market a wide range of products from different channel partners may prefer to develop their own branding rather than adopt a brand that only represents part of their customer offering.

Developing a Distribution Channel Strategy

A distribution channel strategy enables you to sell to customers in geographical areas or market sectors that your direct sales team cannot reach. You can choose from a number of distribution channels, including wholesalers, retailers, distributors and the Internet. Each channel gives you different options for dealing with customers and prospects. However, to ensure that your distributors operate effectively on your behalf, your strategy must incorporate the right level of control and support.

Reach

If your strategy is to grow your business regionally or nationally, highlight the geographical areas you want to reach through a distribution channel and identify a network of distributors or retailers that provide existing coverage of the territories. If you are planning to export products, focus on established distributors with detailed local market knowledge. Consider marketing your products on the Internet so that you can extend coverage to customers where there is no suitable physical distribution network.

Cost

Although a distribution strategy gives you a ready-made platform for expansion, it's important to compare the cost of dealing through indirect distribution channels with the cost of setting up your own network or direct sales operation. Without a distribution network, you will have to commit resources to order processing, stockholding, delivery, invoicing and customer service. Compare that with the lower margins you will make by giving distributors a discount for providing a similar level of service and providing them with a program of marketing and training support.

Contribution

Your strategy should also take account of the potential contribution of each distribution channel. Concentrate on working with distributors that give you access to an additional customer base, with no additional direct sales and marketing costs. Distributors also provide you with local market knowledge, enabling you to establish your business in new markets without incurring heavy market entry costs.

Support

Support and control are critical factors in your distribution strategy. Appointing a manager to work with distributors enables you to monitor their performance and identify their support needs. Develop marketing support programs to meet the needs of different channels. Options include funds for advertising or direct marketing campaigns or templates that enable partners to develop their own campaigns. If channel sales represent a significant proportion of your business, develop advertising and marketing campaigns to drive business to your channel partners. Operating a training program will improve distributors' product and marketing knowledge and enable them to deliver a higher standard of service to customers.

Customer Service

It's important to identify the types of customers you wish to serve directly. Typically, these would be your largest customers or customers that demand levels of technical support beyond your partners' capability. Use channel partners to deal with large numbers of smaller customers cost-effectively so that you can concentrate your resources on your key accounts.

Starting Your Own Network Marketing Business

In order to start your own network marketing company, you can enroll with an existing MLM organization or start your own from the ground up. Network marketing or MLM can be a viable opportunity, provided the emphasis is placed on selling products rather than signing up new members. In order to start your own network marketing company you can enroll with an existing MLM organization or start your own from the ground up, but if you go the DIY route you'll need to establish a relationship with a wholesaler or manufacturer to turn out your actual product.

Find a Niche

Select a product line for your network marketing company. Start a nutritional network marketing company, for example, which is the most popular type of network marketing business.

Wholesale Suppliers

Call several potential wholesale and manufacturer suppliers. Ask them if they offer drop-shipping services, which will keep your inventory levels down. Find out if the supplier offers catalogs, brochures and order forms for their products. Choose the supplier that provides you with the lowest unit cost per product.

Set Price Structure
Set the retail price of your products according to your supplier's recommendations. Establish a commission structure for your distributors on several different levels. Set commissions at 10 percent, for example, for first-level sales where distributors earn money off those people they recruit. Set commissions on levels two and three at 5 percent each, for example, allowing distributors to earn commissions off people your distributors recruit.

Organizational and Management Setup
Install network marketing commission-payment software. Use your commission-payment software to calculate the commissions of all future distributors.
Create an instruction manual for all distributors, highlighting various ways to advertise their network marketing businesses. Create a distributor's kit for all potential dealers, which includes the instruction manual, a catalog, price list and order forms.

How to Advertise and Market Your Business
Advertise your network marketing company in major business opportunity magazines, including "Business Opportunities," "Home Business" and "Small Business Opportunities." Start with classified ads as they are the most cost-effective of all ads.
Mail a sales letter brochure and order form out to people who respond to your classified ads. Call people back when they inquire about your network marketing opportunity. Recruit distributors into your business on an ongoing basis.
Create a website and include your website in your classified advertisements. This will give people another way to join your network marketing opportunity. Get a merchant account through your bank so you can accept credit cards online. Find a web designer if you are unable to create your own website. Have the web designer create self-replicating sites for your distributors so they can recruit their own distributors. Self-replicating sites will have the same URL or address as your site, but with unique extensions or identification numbers. The success of any networking marketing company is contingent upon building a deep organizational structure.

Items you will need
- Wholesale supplier
- Commission payment software
- Instruction manual
- Catalogs
- Sales letters
- Brochures
- Price lists
- Order forms
- Shipping envelopes or boxes
- Shipping labels

Things Needed
- Wholesale supplier
- Commission payment software
- Instruction manual
- Catalogs
- Sales letters
- Brochures
- Price lists
- Order forms
- Shipping envelopes or boxes
- Shipping labels

Tips
Create a website and include your website in your classified advertisements. This will give people another way to join your network marketing opportunity. Get a merchant account through your bank so you can accept credit cards online. Find a web designer if you are unable to create your own website. Have the web designer create self-replicating sites for your distributors so they can recruit their own distributors. Self-replicating sites will have the same URL or address as your site, but with unique extensions or identification numbers. The success of any networking marketing company is contingent upon building a deep organizational structure.

Chapter 2
The 7 Commandments
Of Network Marketing Leaderships

Network Marketing is all about leadership development. To really succeed at a high level, you need the ability to identify existing leaders, recognize upcoming potential leaders, and then help those potential leaders step into their greatness.

Not only must you lead your team, but you must eventually step aside and make room for new leaders to emerge and take over your role. Your job is to work yourself out of a job.

The author of this book spent 25 years working and analyzing these processes, He quantified them into seven leadership laws. To truly become a great leader in the Network Marketing profession, you have to be in accordance with all of these laws. Not only must you work in accord with them, but you must live your life in accord with them:

Leadership Law #1:

The First Person You Lead is Yourself

When I was a year or two into the business, I was complaining to my sponsor about my team. Most of them were lazy, never brought guests to the meetings, and just wanted to wait around for their group to make them rich. I wondered why they couldn't be more like me.

Unfortunately, they were. That was the problem.

I had made the classic mistake of many beginners in Network Marketing: thinking that you can sponsor a few people and then manage them into making you rich.

Sorry, that dog doesn't hunt.

As it pointed out in this book, making the First Circle Work, it's really about personal responsibility. Because our business is one of modeling behavior. It doesn't really matter what you tell your people; what they're really taking note of is what you do. You're never really off the display. They notice if you bring guests, sponsor new people, attend events, and follow the system. They study how you respect and edify the sponsorship line (or don't). They watch how you handle problems, interact with the company, and speak about others when they're not around.

You are responsible for going first, testing the way, finding what works, and then sharing that information down the group.

(Although hopefully you have a sponsorship line that has done much of that, and your response is more about teaching and perpetuating the existing system of duplication.)

Success requires you be a unique amalgamation of mentor, coach, teacher, commanding officer, and partner. People don't work for you, they work for themselves, but of course, what they do impacts your own results and income.

This requires a delicate dance of supervision, training, demonstrating, and leading by example. And that's not something you're going to learn in your distributor kit.

In fact, the best training I ever got for Network Marketing didn't come from Network Marketing.

What helped me more than anything else was the work I did running political campaigns, serving on my condo board, and being president of the Chamber of Commerce, the local chapter of the speakers association, and my church board? Because in each case I was working with an all-volunteer army. When you can't hire and fire people, you're forced to learn how to inspire, lead, and partner for a common goal.

And all leadership starts by example:
You have to prove you are capable to lead yourself first before you can expect anyone else to decide to follow you. And the paradoxical thing is that when you control your own actions, it actually influences the actions of your whole team. You cause the certain behavior to happen and a culture to be formed, but you do it by modeling the behavior yourself and being the example people decide to duplicate.

Leadership Lesson:
When you're ready to lead, start with the person in the mirror.

Leadership Law #2:
You Grow Your People, and They Grow the Network
You can't actually grow your network, no one can. Networks are constantly morphing organizations, made up of many divergent kinds of people, culture, work habits, systems, and philosophy. The individual

actions of the majority become the driving factor of what the network does.

And that starts with personal growth:
One of the things he has been saying for more than twenty years now is – your business will grow only as fast as you do. Everything you do to grow yourself somehow helps your business grow.
Learning a foreign language, taking a philosophy class in night school, or even studying yoga will cause good things to happen in your biz. There is an osmosis that takes place as you grow in any area that transfers to other areas.
You develop confidence, poise, wisdom, knowledge, and skills. All of these things make you more attractive to prospects and increases the respect you receive from your team.
The key is creating a culture of personal growth in your team.
It's not enough to tell your people to read positive books or listen to positive audios. Truth is, most people don't even know what that means. If you have a structured self-development program for your team, you'll see dramatically better results. Things like a book of the month program or subscription series for audios work amazingly well.

Leadership Lesson:
Just like your own growth grows your business, the growth of the individual people on your team is what causes your network to grow.

Leadership Law #3:
You Don't Manage People – You Lead People and Manage Things
One of the big problems in Network Marketing is the terms companies adopt for rank advancements. They love to give people titles like Manager, Directors, and Supervisors. And these are usually for entry-level ranks.
So what happens?
Someone sponsors four people and becomes a "Manager." Now they want to stop recruiting and "manage" their team. Or they have ten team members, which makes them a "Supervisor." Now they think it's all about supervising their group instead of actually doing the business.
Network Marketing is not about managing people, it's about leading them. That means setting an example, modeling the behavior and reaching down in the group, guiding and training. About ten years ago he

was asked to contribute a chapter to a book on leadership. They asked me to define it. He said…

Leadership is the ability to cause people to willingly do things; they wouldn't ordinarily want to do.

That's all leadership is in a nutshell. Not forcing people to do things; causing them to want to do things. Especially things they normally wouldn't want to do.

We often look to the military for leadership examples, because the examples are so compelling. Someone decides to charge a machine gun nest, throw themselves on a grenade, or take some other heroic action to save their unit or innocent civilians. That doesn't happen without strong, powerful leadership from the field leaders, perhaps even up to the head of State.

Now obviously we don't need such dramatic actions from people in our business. But when you lead the team adroitly, you do cause them to decide to do things they didn't want to do when they first joined the business. These can range from buying and wearing their first tie, hosting their first home meeting, or speaking in front of a large crowd.

Leadership Lesson:
Manage the things: authorships, event attendance, volume, training, etc. But when it comes to your people – lead them.

Leadership Law #4:
True Leaders Don't Develop People's Belief in the Leader — They Develop Belief in the Followers

Many people think leadership is about creating confidence and belief in them as a leader. Demagogues may do this, but they're not really advancing the cause. Leaders, who make a positive difference, build the belief and confidence in the people who follow them – in themselves.

Leadership Lesson:
Don't sell your team on what a great leader you are. Sell them on their own ability to have more, do more, and become more. Build their belief in their own unique abilities to be great, and you will truly be a great leader.

Leadership Law #5:
If You Ask Everyone to Lead — No One Does
You probably heard about the study regarding human behavior when a large crowd witnessed a mugging. No one called the police because there were so many bystanders; everyone assumed someone else was doing it. There's a similar dynamic about leadership in Network Marketing, and it leads us to what is probably the biggest mistake people make in the business...

They assume everyone that joins the business is a leader or wants to become a leader, so they treat everyone as a one.

Big mistake
Nothing kills the growth of a team faster. Here's why:
Go collect 100 people from any downtown street. Probably five of them have leadership potential and desire. The other 95 percent are much happier being followers.
Now in our business, the numbers are usually higher if you're doing a good job with your marketing efforts. You're attracting entrepreneurs and people with entrepreneurial aspirations, so you may have 10 or even 15 percent of your team with leadership potential.
That still leaves you with 85 percent.

They don't want to lead. They're afraid to lead. And they don't want the responsibility that leadership entails. They love the products or services, they want to earn enough to cover their cost, and they may be happy with a few hundred dollars a month in additional income.
They can get these benefits with a minimal amount of effort, so they're happy in this situation. Don't make leadership behavior the cost of entry. If you do, it will cause two things to happen.

1. You disempower many potential leaders because they think everyone else is handling the leadership functions; and,
2. You scare away the 85 presenters, because they don't actually want to be leaders.

Don't set up your system and training expecting that everyone who joins the business is a leader. Know that many people will join the business simply because they like the products and want to get them at wholesale. Others will join thinking they are going to be big builders, but when Tuesday night rolls around, they're not going to make it out of the house because the remote control is beckoning them. Others will stay involved simply because they like being around positive people at the events.

Some people will stay in your business because they love the recognition they get for setting up beautiful product displays. Others will stay because you have a talent show at the convention every year and that's their chance to show off their Karaoke skills. Yet others hang around because you have nachos or cookies at the events.

If you berate, belittle, or humiliate these people because they're not willing to do leadership activities you simply drive them out of the business. And a network with 15 percent leaders and no 85 percent of followers will quickly turn into no network at all.

When you leave the judgment aside and just let people participate at the level they're comfortable with, they hang around a lot longer. And if you keep them hanging around the team, there's a good chance that somewhere down the road they will decide they're ready to be a leader.

Leadership Lesson:
You need the whole spectrum: leaders, followers, and product users. Let everyone self-select what category they want to belong to.

Leadership Law #6
Leaders Nurture and Celebrate the Success of their Followers
You're in business for yourself and have a responsibility for it. You have goals you set, ranks you reach, and other benchmarks that tell you when you're on or off track. This can make you become self-centered and take you down the wrong path.

One of the things capable leaders do is measure, monitor, and modulate their progress by using benchmarks of people on their team.

Instead of focusing on just your rank advancement, think about getting five of your personal enrollees to their next rank. Doing this will certainly help your own advancement, and it will do it better. Because there will be a stronger foundation underlying your progress. Zig Ziglar's been saying it for 40 years: If you help enough people get what they want; you'll get what you want.

And it should go without saying, but won't, leaders don't fear their people's progress or get jealous of it. They celebrate it!

For five years in a row, I was the top income earner in my company. By the third year in my acceptance speech, I said I wanted one of my team members to take it from me the next year. And while some came close, no one unseated me.

Then earlier this year, for one month, one of my personal Diamond Directors was the top earner, beating me out. It couldn't have been happier. Our goal is to have at least five of my personals earning more than me.

Which of course would probably combine to make us the top income earner again.

And then we will work again to get at least five earning more than me. And continue the vicious cycle of abundance.

Leadership Lesson:
Recognize and celebrate the achievements of your team, and there will always be more to recognize and celebrate.

Leadership Law #7

The True Test of a Leader is Not How Many Followers You Have – It is How Many Leaders You Develop

This is much related to law number four. And in no business is this more vital than Network Marketing. In our biz, it's all about developing leaders. For maximum duplication, you need to have the next generation of leaders coming up the ranks every few months.

So don't get seduced with numbers like the number of people in a line or the total number of people on your team. These statistics do have value. But they're not nearly as important as how many leaders are in a line and on your team as a whole. That means giving up the need to always be in control, do all the presentations and conduct all the training events.

It means allowing developing leaders to make mistakes.

And they will make mistakes. And they'll be doing things sometimes that maybe you could do better. But if you don't let your people attempt new things and learn and grow through mistakes, you'll always have to do everything.

If you help your followers develop the belief in themselves, a greater number will graduate into leaders. And that's where the real breakthroughs live!

Leadership Lesson:
Your real criteria should be never to do something for a team member that they are capable of doing themselves.

Share the Information
Spreading the word and circulate it to everyone on your team and others you know in the profession.

It's time we came together as a profession. Instead of fighting over the pie, we can lock arms to build a bigger pie. That's the real leadership lesson for us all. We need to stop competing with each other and compete instead with the broken economic model in the rest of the business world.

Government entitlement programs, socialistic policies, and corporate greed are tearing the structure apart. We've lost our way. We must get back to the principles of hard work, integrity and fair competition. We must get back to operating on the principles of free enterprise.

There will always be people that leave one network marketing company and decide another is a better fit for them. That's natural and there's nothing wrong with that. But we have to stop attacking other companies and concentrating our recruiting efforts of trying to pirate distributors from other companies.

Tearing down another company does not make your company look better. In fact, it diminishes us all. Network Marketing is creating a revolution in the business world today. It has never had more recognition in mainstream media, acceptance from government regulators, and fascination from the public. We need to build on this and move forward.

But to reach that goal, we have to work together as a profession, competing fairly with each other with good sportsmanship, ethics, and professionalism. Mass acceptance won't come by shuffling distributors between companies but reaching the people that aren't in our profession yet.

There are more than six billion people in the world who aren't in Network Marketing yet. That's where the tipping point is. And to reach that level will require stronger leadership. Good luck!

Chapter 3
Choosing your Network Marketing Business

When contemplating entering any business it is important to do your homework, to determine the viability of that business and whether it is the right one for you. This first section covers a number of topics that you should consider as part of your decision-making process before becoming involved in network marketing. The message that shines through is that you can never do too much homework on any company that you are looking to work with. The more comfortable you feel with the company, the more commitment you will have and the more successful your business will be. If you are already involved, this section will also be valuable in reaffirming your decision or highlighting something that you had not taken into consideration previously.

- #1 Finding the right network marketing business for you
- #2 The good, the bad and the downright ugly
- #3 Networking versus pyramid schemes
- #4 Take your time and do your homework
- #5 Always get your information from a credible source
- #6 Anyone can succeed in network marketing
- #7 Many fail, but many succeed in a big way
- #8 There will always be hurdles to overcome

#1 Finding the right network marketing business for you
For the majority of people, their introduction to network marketing has been through an invitation by someone already involved in a particular company, and therefore their only decision has been whether or not to get involved, rather than which company to get involved with. Today though, due to the growing positive exposure that network marketing is getting around the world, people are initiating contact through their own interest and desire to know more, and seeking out companies they would like to be affiliated with.

Network marketing and its acceptance are growing, with an increasing number of network marketing companies operating globally. Their business models, structures, cultures, products, and remuneration can vary considerably; it is important to understand this variation rather than thinking of them as all the same.

For instance, you may have a background in the health industry or take a keen interest in your own health and wellbeing. A network marketing company that specializes in health or has a large product category in this industry may be best suited to you. It may be that your passion is for the beauty industry; again, a company that either specializes in or carries beauty products will be where you can take your passion and make a business of your own. For some, it may be professional or specialized services, for others a company that offers a large cross-section of products and services. Other considerations could be that some network marketing company's suit your time availability better or that another's remuneration structure best suits your goals and dreams. It may be that you are looking for the security of a more established company, or the ground-floor opportunities that newly established companies provide.

Whatever the reason, with so much choice, it is important that you do your homework and find the company that's right for you.

#2 The good, the bad and the downright ugly
In all industries, there are the good companies and not so good companies, the reputable and not so reputable, the ethical and not so ethical. This applies equally to network marketing organizations, although, as we discussed in the introduction, the industry has come a long way in recent years, and corporate compliance regulations in most countries require and enforce the highest of ethics and standards. Most of the today's network marketing companies sell quality products—if they didn't, they simply would not be able to remain in business. What is really important is to make sure the company is credible. Due to the growing acceptance of network marketing, more and more network marketing companies are being established.

The majority are legitimate but some others, recognizing the trend, try to disguise themselves as a network marketing system when in fact they may be a pyramid scheme; still, others are planning to be in the market for only a short time, make their money from the unsuspecting, and then disappear. Remembering that the aim of building a successful network marketing business is to establish a long-term passive income, it is very important that you feel the company you are joining is going to be around for the long term. Even though the 'ground-floor opportunity' promoted by a newly established company is often attractive; much can be said for the company that has been around for a long time. Longevity within the network marketing industry is a sign of stability, credibility, a sound business model, proven systems and, most importantly, a commitment to the independent business owner's long-term profitability.

This is certainly not to suggest that newly formed network marketing companies are not legitimate but to point out that those companies that have been established over the long term have the advantage of offering a sense of security and confidence to those thinking of affiliating with them, as compared to a new company with an unproven record.

So satisfy yourself; do your own research. Talk to other people who are involved, ring the head office or ideally visit it. Buy some of the products to satisfy yourself that they are high quality; in general, do whatever you can to be certain that this is an organization you would like to be associated with. Don't believe everything you read, especially when it is online. Don't be pressured into joining any organization. If you have any nagging doubts, listen to the little voice inside you. It will soon become fairly clear which network marketing businesses really are credible and can back up their offers and claims, and which ones to steer clear of—but in the end, it is entirely up to you and to your own due diligence and research.

#3 Networking versus pyramid schemes

For the uninitiated there is a risk of unwittingly getting involved in a pyramid scheme, thinking it is network marketing. Unfortunately, because of the growth of the network marketing industry, there will always be pyramid schemes around who will go out of their way to disguise themselves as a network marketing company. Due to a crackdown in recent times, these schemes are not as active as they once were, and the risk to the unsuspecting has been minimized.

There are many government organizations and watchdogs that can offer advice on pyramid schemes; a simple online search will give you the right organization to contact in your country or state. Please take the time to do this. Pyramid schemes are often extremely convincing and attractive, but they are unethical and illegal. Generally, the person at the top of the pyramid makes a pile of money and the people at the bottom lose most of theirs.

Pyramid schemes often target people they know who are in network marketing businesses simply because they already have a network they are selling to. Plus they are generally open-minded and they are motivated to get results.

If an opportunity looks too good to be true, it probably is. Network marketing businesses can make you a lot of money, but getting there takes time, energy and conviction. They are not an overnight path to fabulous fame and fortune, which is generally how pyramid schemes are sold to the unsuspecting.

#4 Take your time and do your homework

When deciding whether to get involved in network marketing or which company to be involved with, be sure that you give yourself enough time to make an informed decision. Be careful neither to make an off-the-cuff decision and jump straight in nor to dismiss the opportunity without checking it out. Whether it takes you a week, a month or a year, take the time to properly research the opportunity. A word of warning, though: be careful that you are not simply procrastinating on getting started due to a fear of the unknown or because you are being influenced by the opinions of others.

It is important that you feel comfortable with your decision; don't be railroaded by someone 'selling you on the idea'. People who are railroaded rarely go on to build a successful business. A key to building any successful business is to be excited and passionate about what you do. With so many different network marketing companies now providing a vast array of different products and services, it is important that you find the one that is right for you, the one that you are excited about. When you are doing your homework, take the same approach that you'd use if you were looking to start a traditional business.

If you are looking to make a start in network marketing, use the following series of questions as a framework or reference point which you can come back to. Note down what you like about the opportunity being offered, and what you find challenging, and compare the results to assist you in your decision-making process. If you are already involved in the industry, still note down what you like and what you find challenging about what you are doing, and discuss your pointers with your support team.

1) What do I like about the opportunity?
2) What do I find challenging about the opportunity?
3) What homework have I done?
4) Do I have any nagging doubts that I would like answered?

#5 Always get your information from a credible source

Far too often someone looking at a network marketing opportunity will seek the advice of people who are simply not qualified to give it. Nearly everyone has some opinion or other on network marketing, but when you challenge them, you will find that a large majority have no real knowledge of the industry or how it works. You must be very careful when researching your involvement and looking for more information that you seek it from someone who is qualified to provide it. The person who best fits these criteria is someone who has been successful in the industry.

When seeking information, ask yourself: Is this person qualified to be offering this information? Have they been successful in network marketing? Have they been successful in any of their endeavors? Are they entrepreneurial? Are they financially independent? Or are they struggling financially and going through life on a treadmill?

Some people will say that information or advice from someone who has been successful in network marketing must inevitably be biased. Others, the smart ones, will see it as common sense. If you wanted to really lose weight, is it best to get advice on how to do that from someone who has tried and failed, or from someone who has been successful? If you wanted to establish a successful traditional business, would you seek the advice of someone who has failed or someone who has been successful?

A word of warning on researching via the Internet. While the Internet is a great tool for accessing information, be aware that it also provides a platform for anyone to put unqualified information and negative comments on any subject, including network marketing. If you are using the Internet for research, do not let yourself be influenced by such comments without first being sure of the credibility of the source.

The Internet can provide you with lots of valuable information, but at the same time, it contains just as much valueless nonsense. You need to be sure that you can determine which is which. In the end, you need to be certain that the decisions you make are not governed by information and advice given by unqualified people.

#6 Anyone can succeed in network marketing
Two common questions are 'Can I do it?' and 'Am I the right type of person?' the answers are 'Yes, you can' and 'Yes, you are'. That said, the journey in building a network marketing business is different for each person. Some already come with certain skills, experience, and confidence that will make it easier for them, while others come with little in the way of skills, experience, and confidence, which may create some challenges. What's important to understand is that both types of person can be successful, even though the journey and the time it takes will vary.

Take, for example, the story of two totally different couples who started in the same network marketing company. Rose and Rud had professional backgrounds; both were well-educated and very successful in their chosen fields. They were well-respected, had a good network of family and friends and had credibility. Robin and Rufa were from a lower socioeconomic background. They had only basic education and had struggled financially most of their lives. They had only a small network of family and friends and lacked credibility.

The two couples started their network marketing businesses around the same time. Each had their own reasons for getting involved. Each had dreams they wanted to achieve that their current situation could not deliver to them. Even though their backgrounds were vastly different, there were two things that made them equal—both had a dream, and both had a desire to learn whatever was needed to make a success of their business and achieve that dream.

Rose and Rud's business grew quickly because the couple already had an awareness of success principles and the added advantage of credibility when talking to others about the opportunity. Robin and Rufa's start was a lot slower due to not having been exposed to success principles before and their significant lack of credibility in the eyes of those they talked with.

Nonetheless, both couples went on to build very successful businesses, the only difference being the time each took to achieve that success.

Both couples have now been successfully running their network marketing businesses for a number of years and both have gone on to achieve the dreams that they aspired to. Do you think that Robin and Rufa really believe it matters that it took them longer than Rose and Ruds? Maybe it did at the time, but now, after so many years of the lifestyle they enjoy, the time it took to get the job done has paled into insignificance.

Network marketing provides a great level playing field. Those involved may be tradespeople or professionals, educated or uneducated, shy or outgoing, but in the industry everyone is equal and everyone can succeed. What is most important is to understand that everything required to make a success of your network marketing business can be learned, but the desire to learn is essential if you want your business to grow quickly.

#7 Many fail, but many succeed in a big way

If you've never met anyone who has been in network marketing and failed, you simply need to get out more. There are countless numbers of people who have failed at network marketing, just as there are countless numbers of people who have failed at weight loss, a fitness program, learning a new musical instrument, learning a new language, finishing university or, more to the point, traditional business. Does this mean that no one can ever lose weight, get fit, and learn to play a musical instrument, speak another language, get a university degree or have a successful business? Of course not. The reality is that there will always be a percentage of failures in most endeavors but, as long as there are percentages of success, it is proof that you too can succeed. The level of success and the time is taken to achieve it varies from individual to individual, but if you have the drive, the motivation, the sticking ability and, most importantly, the dream, you can make it work.

So when it comes to choosing your network marketing business, once again we come to the key point of this section— make an informed decision based on all of the information at hand. Find out about the success stories, but also find out about the failures—and why they failed. Collect a complete and accurate view of the business opportunity to make sure it fits with you and where you are in your life.

#8 There will always be hurdles to overcome

Network marketing provides a great business opportunity, but like all businesses, it has its challenges and pitfalls. The scope of these and their impact will vary for each person, with some finding certain areas easier than others. Compared to some of the challenges and pitfalls faced every day by traditional business owners, those faced in network marketing pale into insignificance, but they are there, and it is important that you are aware of them. In particular, it is crucial that you are aware of the ones that relate to you so you can address or avoid them.

Some of the challenges and pitfalls you may face include:

- stepping out of your comfort zone
- negativity from friends and family
- people letting you down
- having to do extra work on top of what you are already doing

- not always achieving your goals
- giving up some leisure time in the short term
- extra strain on your finances in the short term
- frustration that it's not working for you as quickly as you would like.

Everyone who's gone on to build successful network marketing business has had their own challenges to overcome and experienced some pitfalls along the way, but all of them have backed that up with hard work, commitment, persistence and a never-give-up attitude, something also required if you are to be successful in traditional business. For most, the road has not always been easy, but the trip has certainly been worth it. They will all tell you, 'Although it has been challenging at times, compared to what we were doing before network marketing, it has been easy.' Don't fall for any razzle-dazzle. It takes time, energy and money to build any business. Go into it with this knowledge very clear in your mind.

Chapter 4
How to Research a Business Opportunity

Just what is a business opportunity? That question has plagued a great many people trying to decide whether to buy a current independent business, a franchise, or what we'll refer to in this text as a business opportunity. To allay the confusion, we offer a simple analogy. Think back to elementary school when your teacher was explaining the difference between a rectangle and a square. A square is also a rectangle, but a rectangle isn't necessarily a square. The same relationship exists between business opportunities, independent businesses for sale and franchises. All franchises and independent businesses for sale are business opportunities, but not all business opportunities meet the requirement of being a franchise nor are they in the strictest sense of the word independent businesses for sale.

Making matters even more confusing is the fact that 26 states have passed laws defining business opportunities and regulating their sales. Often these statutes are drafted so comprehensively that they include franchises as well.

Not every state with a business opportunity law defines the term in the same manner. However, most of them use the following general criteria to define one:

1. A business opportunity involves the sale or lease of any product, service, equipment, etc. that will enable the purchaser-licensee to begin a business.

2. The licensor or seller of a business opportunity declares that it will secure or assist the buyer in finding a suitable location or provide the product to the purchaser-licensee.

3. The licensor-seller guarantees an income greater than or equal to the price the licensee-buyer pays for the product when it's resold and that there is a market presence for the product or service.

4. The initial fee paid to the seller in order to start the business opportunity must range between $400 and $1,000.

5. The licensor-seller promises to buy back any product purchased by the licensee-buyer in the event it cannot be sold to the prospective customers of the business.

6. Any products or services developed by the seller-licensor will be purchased by the licensee-buyer.

7. The licensor-seller of the business opportunity will supply a sales or marketing program for the licensee-buyer that many times will include the use of a trade name or trademark.

The laws covering business opportunity ventures usually exclude the sale of an independent business by its owner. Rather, they are meant to cover the multiple sales of distributorships or businesses that do not meet the requirements of a franchise under the Federal Trade Commission (FTC) rule passed in 1979. This act defines business offerings in three formats: package franchises, product franchises and business opportunity ventures.

In order to be a business opportunity venture under the FTC rule, four elements must be present:

1. The individual who buys a business opportunity, often referred to as a licensee or franchisee, must distribute or sell goods or services supplied by the licenser or franchisor.

2. The licensor or franchisor must help secure a retail outlet or accounts for the goods and services the licensee is distributing or selling.

3. There must be a cash transaction between the two parties of at least $500 prior to or within six months after the licensee or franchisee starts the business venture.

4. All terms and conditions of the relationship between the licensor and the licensee must be stated in writing.

You can readily see that the sale of business opportunities as defined by the FTC rule is quite different from the sale of an independent business. When you're dealing with the sale of an independent business, the buyer has no obligations to the seller. Once the sales transaction is completed, the buyer can subscribe to any business operations system he or she prefers. There is no continued relationship required by the seller. Business opportunity ventures, like franchises, are businesses in which the seller makes a commitment of continuing involvement with the buyer.

Types of Business Opportunities

The FTC describes the most common types of business opportunity ventures as follows:

- **Distributorship.** Refers to an independent agent that has entered into an agreement to offer and sell the product of another but is not entitled to use the manufacturer's trade name as part of its trade name. Depending on the agreement, the distributor may be limited to selling only that company's goods or it may have the freedom to market several different product lines or services from various firms.

- **Rack jobber.** Involves the selling of another company's products through a distribution system of racks in a variety of stores that are serviced by the rack jobber. Typically, the agent or buyer enters into an agreement with the parent company to market their goods to various stores by means of strategically located store racks. The parent company obtains a number of locations in which the racks are placed on a consignment basis. It's up to the agent to maintain the inventory, move the merchandise around to attract the customer, and do the bookkeeping. The agent presents the store manager with a copy of the inventory control sheet which indicates how much merchandise was sold, and then the distributor is paid by the store or location which has the rack-less the store's commission.

- **Vending machine routes.** Very similar to rack jobbing. The investment is usually greater for this type of business opportunity venture since the businessperson must buy the machines as well as the merchandise being vended, but here the situation is reversed in terms of the pay procedure. The vending machine operator must pay the location owner a percentage based on sales. The big secret to any route deal is to get locations in high-foot-traffic areas, and of course, as close to one another as possible. If your locations are spread far apart, you waste time and traveling expenses servicing them.

In addition to the three types of business opportunities listed above, there are four other categories you should be aware of:

- **Dealer.** Similar to a distributor but while a distributor may sell to a number of dealers, a dealer will usually sell only to a retailer or the consumer.
- **Trademark/product licenses.** Under this type of arrangement, the licensee obtains the right to use the seller's trade name as well as specific methods, equipment, technology or products. Use of the trade name is purely optional.

- **Network marketing.** This is a generic term that covers the realm of direct sales and multilevel marketing. As a network marketing agent, you would sell products through your own network of friends, neighbors, co-workers and so on. In some instances, you may gain additional commissions by recruiting other agents.

- **Cooperatives.** This business is similar to a licensee arrangement in which an existing business, such as a hotel or hardware store, can affiliate with a larger network of similar businesses, often for the sole purpose of advertising and promoting through a common identity.

How Government Protects You

The FTC Rule, which has been in effect since the latter part of 1979, has had a broad-ranging impact on the franchise and business opportunity industry and would-be franchisees and licensees. The rule is designed to assure all prospective buyers, of either a franchise or business opportunity that they'll receive a full disclosure containing the type of background information needed to make an informed investment decision.

In spite of the FTC's rule and aggressive action at the state level, there are sellers who seek every possible means to escape regulation. Neither the FTC rule nor state regulations can guarantee freedom from fraud. That's why you should pay especially close attention to the FTC disclosure statement that is presented to you.

Every prospective buyer of a business opportunity must receive the FTC disclosure statement at least 10 business days before signing a binding contract or paying money (or other consideration) to the seller. The 10-business day requirement is minimal. If you meet face-to-face with the licensor or a representative to discuss a proposed sale or purchase of the business opportunity, and if the conversation results in a serous sales presentation, the licensor must provide you with a disclosure document at that time.

If you haven't received an FTC disclosure document, don't sign anything or pay out any money, even if claims are made that it is "refundable."

If the seller doesn't give you a disclosure document, they're violating federal law and may also be violating state law. If the salesperson claims his or her offering is exempt from the FTC requirements, demand to see an opinion letter from counsel before dealing with them any further. Also ask the salesperson for the phone number of the local state agency or FTC office that has advised them they are exempt. Very few business opportunity offerings are exempt. The only major exceptions are those where the total initial payment within the first six months is less than $500, or where payment is made only for initial inventory sold at bona fide wholesale price.

Franchises vs. Business Opportunities

As a rule of thumb, a franchisee receives more support from the parent company, gets to use the trademarked name, and is more stringently controlled by the franchisor. Business opportunities, on the other hand, don't receive as much support from the parent company, generally aren't offered the use of a trademarked name, and are independent of the parent company's operational guidelines.

As we've previously noted, there are numerous forms of business opportunity ventures. Some are even turnkey operations similar to a lot of package-format franchises. These business opportunities provide everything you could possibly need to start a business. They help you select a location, they provide training, they offer support for the licensee's marketing efforts, and they supply a complete start-up inventory.

Unlike a package-format franchise, however, these types of business opportunity ventures aren't trademarked outlets for the parent company. The company's name, logo and how it's legally operated are left solely to the licensee. Many times the only binding requirement between the seller and the buyer is that inventory be purchased solely through the parent company. Of course, all these stipulations are outlined in the disclosure statement and contract.

The Advantages of a Business Opportunity

Requires a lower initial fee than a franchise. Although the number of low-investment franchises has increased, the fee to get into a business opportunity is still considerably lower. The FTC requires a $500 minimum investment for an opportunity to be considered a business opportunity, but there are many that fall under this set fee, although most average around $2,000 to $3,000.

- **A proven system of operation or product.** Existing systems serve to maximize efficiency and returns and minimize problems. It's simply a matter of passing on experience, still the best teacher. Whether they admit it or not, most people like having their hands held once in a while. During crises, the parent company is there to help the licensee over the bumps. Many people like this idea of safety in numbers.

- **Intensive training programs.** In any new business, a lot of time and money are consumed during the learning period. A good business opportunity venture can eliminate the majority of ineffective moves through an intensive training program.

- **Better financing options.** Because of its financial size, credit line and contractual agreements, the parent company offering the business opportunity can often arrange better financing than an individual could obtain. Financial leverage is an important consideration in any investment situation.

- **Professional advertising and promotion.** Most small businesspeople don't spend sufficient money on advertising. When they do, their efforts are often poorly conceived and inconsistent. Many business opportunity ventures supply the buyer with print advertising slicks, radio ads, TV storyboards, etc., in order to provide a better marketing effort. Some business opportunity ventures will even have a cooperative advertising agreement under which they will split the cost of print, radio or TV ads. This type of marketing help is especially beneficial in large metropolitan areas where the cost of media is prohibitive to the one-shop owner.

- **Ongoing counseling.** Most business opportunity ventures offer support not only through training but also through counseling from a staff of experts who offer assistance that no independent could afford. Legal advice is available to a certain degree. The most efficient accounting systems-perfect for that particular business-have been designed by experts in the field. Some licensors offer free computer analysis of records, and through comparison with other units can pinpoint areas of inefficiency or loss as well as profitable aspects of the business that are being neglected.

- **Site selection assistance.** Experts in site selection and marketing choose locations using all the scientific tools available. Professional negotiators arrange leases and contracts to the best advantage, using the power of a large organization to influence landlords and other important figures.

- **Purchasing power.** Many times, the parent company's tremendous buying power and special buying techniques can bring products, equipment and outside services to the licensee at a much lower cost than an independent could ever get.

- **No ongoing royalties.** In a business opportunity, unlike in a franchise, there are no ongoing royalties to pay to the seller. The profits are all yours.

The Disadvantages of a Business Opportunity

Under ideal conditions, business opportunities are a good, low-investment way to get into business with minimum risk and a good chance for success. But nothing in this world is perfect, so here are some problems that can be expected:

- **Poor site selection.** The majority of business opportunities are consumer-oriented retail operations which rely on good location, visibility and easy access to the establishment. Most buyers of business opportunities casually accept the locations chosen for them. DON'T! Look it over thoroughly yourself. You might even hire an outside marketing consultant to evaluate and possibly argue with the parent company's choice. Having better locations could literally mean millions of dollars in profit over the course of 20 years.

- **Lack of ongoing support.** There is usually no requirement for the business opportunity seller to offer ongoing support of any kind. If the seller decides not to supply information or guidelines that could help you once you're in operation, you may not have much recourse available to you.

- **Exclusivity clauses.** Are you restricted to selling only the manufacturer's merchandise? If this is the case and you deviate for any reason whatsoever, you run the risk of the licensor canceling the agreement. If you do buy from other sources, it will be very hard to hide-most parent companies will require you to open your books for examination at predestinated periods of time. Any irregularities will be spotted at these times. Most smart buyers of business opportunities will negotiate the point in the agreement stipulating sources of supply in case product quality is inconsistent.

- **Parent-company bankruptcy.** Another pitfall is the possibility of the parent company overextending itself and going bankrupt. While this is not as serious in a business opportunity as it would be in a franchise, you still run the risk of losing the business because your property contracts may have been financed through the parent company.

You should carefully investigate any business opportunity you're considering. Get a list of operators from the parent company and call them. Have a lawyer look over any agreement drafted by the parent company. Make sure you receive a disclosure statement. Then carefully evaluate the licensor. Don't let anyone hurry you. Make sure a responsible company backs the business opportunity.

Guidelines for Choosing a Business Opportunity

First make sure your business opportunity of choice complies with all business opportunity statutes--which vary from state to state--and is registered in states where required. Next, find out if the business opportunity you're interested in provides an offering prospectus to buyers. If it's a business opportunity that falls under the FTC rule, then it's required to disclose specific information to you.

When choosing a business opportunity, keep in mind that if you buy an opportunity from a company with a sizable number of outlets that's been in business for at least three years, you'll pay more for this established concept that you would for a newer one. If you're considering a more recently established business opportunity, you should check out the parent company's history to evaluate its success and longevity in its particular field of operation.

If you were to ask a business consultant how to evaluate the "right" business opportunity for you, you would probably receive these guidelines:

1. **Make an honest evaluation of yourself and your abilities.**
    - If you've been behind a desk for many years, will you be happy calling on businesspeople and selling them an intangible service?

If you've been a field salesperson for years, will you be satisfied selling snack foods behind a counter?

2. You must run your business enthusiastically.
  - ➤ Will you be happy introducing a new product or an unusual service that the public knows nothing about? Can you generate excitement for an item not nationally advertised?

3. You must have complete knowledge of the product or service with which you are involved.
  - ➤ If the parent company gives you little or no training in technical or management know-how, be wary of the business opportunity. If the licensor-seller has organized all the operating knowledge into a standard operating manual, look with favor upon this business opportunity.

4. Make a market evaluation of the product or service to be offered.
  - ➤ Is the time right to introduce it to the public? Is there a need for this type of item, and what is its potential in relation to competition?

5. Find out how many buyers have been in the business successfully for a respectable period of time.
  - ➤ A legitimate business opportunity will even provide you with phone numbers of other buyers, so you can verify that they're generally satisfied with the opportunity and that the seller is capable of fulfilling his or her promises.

6. Check the training and experience required to run the business properly.
  - ➤ Is there a suitable curriculum of training? What is the scope of training? Does your background fit its requirements?

7. What is the company's profit ratio to sales; to time and service requirements; and to the financial leverage requirements?
  - ➤ Can you make more in another type of business?

8. Do you have to work more hours to make the same amount you do now?
   ➢ Can you invest the same amount in the business opportunity yet operate a larger operation and get a better return on investment?

9. Check with current operators to see how they're making out.
   ➢ Are they happy with their businesses? What problems do they have, if any that are common to all units sold?

10. Research company's history.
   ➢ Is it a new firm with little expertise and experience? Is it an older firm whose regular products have satisfied customers for years? Are the business opportunities all offshoots of their regular business?

11. Is there financial strength and strong credit behind the business opportunity?
   ➢ Can the licensor-seller give you an escrow agreement to deliver a building, equipment, leasehold improvements, inventory, etc., as the unit is made ready for your use? Check out the bank references given by the licensor-seller; discuss the company's financial strength with the appropriate managers.

12. Evaluate the policies and plans of the company with the associations and business groups in which the parent company or seller is involved.

13. The Better Business Bureau will give you a report if others have lodged previous complaints against the company.

14. Having an attorney, accountant or business consultant conduct an in-depth study of the company may be an excellent idea.

15. Visit the headquarters of the licensor-seller.
   ➢ Talk to the personnel and the training director. Visit the original prototype of the business being sold. Evaluate other outlets. Expose yourself to the other outlets' products and services to determine the quality dispensed.

Evaluating a Potential Opportunity

In the preceding section, we outlined numerous things you should do to ensure that you're choosing a venture that will be appropriate for you personally, and will represent a sound investment. It's important that you cover all your bases before signing a contract with the seller. The following are some strategies you should use to protect yourself.

- **Have legal representation.** Your attorney should be present when you're negotiating with the licensor-seller. At the very least, your attorney should go over the contract to purchase the business opportunity and advise you as to whether or not you should sign it in its present condition. He or she should explain what each aspect of the contract means so that you understand what you're signing.

- **Have financial representation.** Your accountant should look over the financial statements of the licensor-seller. In addition, he or she should be able to check out the financial strength of the company and determine whether the business is a viable financial investment for you.

- **Make your own independent survey of other owners of business opportunities sold by the parent company.** Are they happy with the company? Did the company do everything it promised? Is the company good to work with? Does it give its distributors help? Does it send out advertising materials? What do they feel are the strengths of the opportunity? If they had to do it over again, would these licensees buy another unit? Would they advise you to buy a unit?

- **Contact competitors.** This will verify the status of the company in the industry. A competing company will tell you in a hurry what the company's weaknesses are. You'll also get an opportunity to see whether or not the business opportunity compares favorably in terms of pricing and so on.

- **Check the credit of the seller.** Your accountant or the person auditing the business opportunity can help you with this. Be sure you understand everything you're signing. Read the disclosure statement, the purchase agreement and the advertising bulletins carefully.

- **Check the credibility of the parent company.** The parent company doesn't have to be big in terms of dollars to be credible. Use your common sense and advice from people you trust to determine whether or not a company seems credible. In many cases, small companies are a great investment for a buyer because you generally deal with the president or the top people in the company. They are going to be training you and working with you. This is a tremendous advantage, as opposed to working with somebody five or six rungs down the ladder who may be just doing a job. Are the seller's people truly interested in you? Do they seem to be sincere? Did they check you out thoroughly? Are they concerned with the kind of buyer that will be carrying their banner? This is very important. If they're just interested in taking your money, you're in trouble.

- **Check the performance of the parent company.** Are the seller's claims backed by performance? Do the claims that the seller make when advertising their product, for example, stand up at the store level? Do the current operators you've talked to confirm the profit claims that the seller makes?
- **Check the company's management.** It's not enough that they've got a good idea. Do they have the management strength to be able to train you, help you and keep the company running for another 20 years?

- **Know all the costs and obligations, both yours and the seller's.** What costs are you going to have to incur? What are your obligations on an ongoing basis? Is the company going to train you? Is training at your own expense? In most cases, you have to pay your own expenses to the training site. How long will the training last? Do you have enough money to sustain yourself while you're in training and before your business starts earning money? What kind of ongoing supervision will the company give you?

- **Determine what type of advertising program is available from the licensor.** Will that advertising program work for you? Check your local market. For instance, if you're buying a business opportunity in which you'll be selling bathtub liners, will advertising in trade magazines really help? Also, what are their ads like? Is the copy good? What about visual art? Don't negate the possibility that their advertising program will hurt you more than it will help. Just because you're dealing with a company that has experience in the field, their marketing campaigns aren't necessarily going to be successful.

- **Are you getting value for your initial purchase price?** Examine the list of equipment, fixtures, inventory, operating supplies, etc. and call a few suppliers dealing in these items. Compare the prices those suppliers quote you against the business opportunity's prices. You may be able to purchase everything, including the inventory, for less money yourself than you could by affiliating with the licensor.

What the Disclosure Statement Tells You

A disclosure statement is a document that contains everything there is to know about the business opportunity and the seller's company. It includes the promoter's financial strength, how many operating units there are, and exactly what you're going to be required to pay in total so there are no hidden fees. The purpose of the disclosure statement is to protect the licensee as well as the licensor and to eliminate some unscrupulous licensors.

As already mentioned, some 26 states have legal requirements for disclosure statements and registration. In addition, there are also federal laws regarding business opportunities. The most significant is the FTC rule requiring full disclosure of the business opportunity on a national level. The rule doesn't require a registration, but it does require a disclosure that follows a specific format.

Most states that have disclosure requirements parallel the federal standards of information that must be supplied to the buyer. In addition, state-required disclosure statements often include information stating that the buyer has three to seven days referred to as a "cooling off" period so the purchaser/investor can reconsider the subject after being bombarded by sales pitches from slick salespeople.

When reviewing a disclosure statement, be aware of the following items:

- **The licensor.** The history of the parent company needs to be detailed. It should include the identity and business experience of any persons affiliated with the licensor, whether the company has been involved in any litigation, whether it or any of the officials in the company have ever declared bankruptcy, any other initial payment or any payment in total, and any other fees.

- **Obligations of the licensee.** If there are any financing arrangements, they have to be stated. If you are going to be required to buy from any supplier, that should be stated up front. The disclosure statement also states what the parent company will have to provide in terms of equipment, training, ongoing services and a training manual.

- **What the licensor promises to deliver.** This should include whether you're getting an exclusive area or territory as a licensee. Any trademarks, service marks, trade names, logo types and commercial symbols as well as any patents or copyrights which you're going to be able to use as a licensee need to be identified in here.

- **Obligation of the licensee.** This is how you will participate in the actual operation of the business opportunity. If this is an absentee business, it must be stated. If the licensor indicates that you must personally operate the business, which should also be stated. Restrictions on goods and services offered by the licensee are covered. It has some provisions for renewal and termination, repurchase and modification. It also has to list the current licensees and their addresses so you have the opportunity to contact these people.

- **Public-figure relationships.** If this is a business opportunity that is identified with a given public figure like a celebrity or athlete, it should indicate what arrangements have been made with that person. Is that person active in the business or receiving a royalty out of the proceeds?

- **Financial statements of the company.** This is required in almost every state. It is an audited financial statement prepared by a CPA. There is usually a letter from the accountant indicating that the books have been audited and are available for people to study. Any estimates or projections of earnings would have to be part of the disclosure statement.

Analyzing the Financial Statements

Profit and loss statements are part of the financing process. In business offerings, these are usually statements audited by a CPA. When you look at a licensor, you'll want to see an audited statement of the company's earnings. You'll know you're getting a legitimate financial statement because CPAs will not stamp a statement that hasn't been properly audited and certified.

You should have an accountant look at the financial statement and interpret exactly what the statement represents for you. You should compare statements from at least two years to see the direction in which the company is moving: Is it on an upswing or a downswing? Is it becoming more profitable and more efficient? The balance sheet, which shows the company's assets and liabilities, is another yardstick with which to determine the strength of a company. The profit-and-loss statement tells you how much money the company is making or losing. The balance sheet tells you what the company is worth in terms of assessing a company's strength.

Companies may give you pro forma projections to show what you can expect to earn in this particular business opportunity. A pro forma is a projected financial statement. It is developed by taking the typical costs for a unit doing $200,000, $300,000 or $400,000 a year and showing you approximately what you can expect to earn at each of those sales levels. Some states have outlawed the use of pro-forma statements except in the case of current operating units. In terms of their reliability, they do not always accurately reflect earning potential.

We recommend examining actual audited operating statements to get a good feel for what this company is doing. Larger companies will be able to provide you with these. Smaller companies usually can't, and that's where a gamble is involved. This is where you have to use your own personal accounting and legal assistance in order to thoroughly check out a company.

Chapter 5
Remember that it is a Business

When you become involved in network marketing it is important that you understand that it is a business, a point reiterated throughout this book. Many people in network marketing never quite grasp the correlation between owning a network marketing business and owning a traditional business. Even though the way each goes about doing business can be vastly different, the basic principle that network marketing is a business never changes.

To build any successful business requires an understanding of a number of basic principles followed up with commitment and good business practices. In this section we look at some topics that will set the foundations for you to go on and build a successful network marketing business.

Treat it like a business, not a hobby.

An important aspect of this book is helping you understand that the elements of building and operating your network marketing business are no different to those of building and operating a traditional business. Most importantly, we aim to help you understand and reinforce that you are in a very real business, not just a hobby.

With this in mind, it is important that you treat your network marketing business as it deserves to be treated. A large number of people who undertake network marketing treat it like a bit of a hobby or something to dabble in, which is okay if you only want hobby results. Those who get involved for the bigger picture will be disappointed and frustrated if they don't approach it in a committed way or give it the respect it needs.

If you have become involved in network marketing in order to build a profitable business, then the first step towards achieving results is to make a conscious decision to treat your new enterprise as a real business—right from day one. Not having a shop front or a factory or a big office takes away nothing from the business itself, and in fact is really smart, as overheads of that kind are what kill many businesses.

Your business has the potential to have a multimillion dollar turnover if that is what you wish, but that won't happen if you operate it with a hobby attitude. We talk about setting goals and dreams later in the book, where we make the point that you can build your network marketing business to give you exactly what it is you want out of life. Treat it as an opportunity that can be as big or as small as you want—but regardless of the size, treat it as a business and you will be well on the way to achieving your desired goals.

Make a commitment and your chances of success will increase.
If you had just started your own traditional business it would be fair to assume that you would be devoting to it a considerable level of commitment, financially, physically and mentally.
Understanding that your network marketing business is just that, a business, be sure that you devote the same level of commitment to it—not just to the network marketing company you are affiliated with or to the person who introduced you, although both are important, but to yourself and your business.

Far too often we see people who get involved in network marketing making the mistake of short-changing themselves when it comes to their level of commitment. The result is a sense of frustration that the business does not seem to be working, or is not working quickly enough, illustrated by the story of John and Jessica, who got involved in network marketing and were keen to get the job done as quickly as possible so that they could give up their jobs. Unfortunately, not long after they got started it became apparent that their commitment did not back up their goal. Soon John and Jessica began to make excuses about not being able to do the things that were suggested to them.

They didn't attend business meetings and seminars, avoided the purchase of support tools and personal development materials, and weren't actively working their business consistently enough to achieve the desired result. Needless to say, this lack of commitment was reflected in the lack of success of their business, and their goal of giving up work as quickly as possible had to be put off.
Your business will require a certain amount of commitment from you in areas like time, effort and finance. Although these commitments are minimal compared to the requirements of a traditional business, they are there nonetheless. By making a commitment, you minimize dithering:

'Will I do this, will I do that, will I attend that meeting, that seminar, do I really want to go out tonight, can I afford this, can I afford that?' By making a commitment you have already answered the question and so you just do it.

Understanding the Universal Laws of Business

If you are new to network marketing, have never been in business before, and you are finding some aspects challenging, ask yourself: 'Would this be any different if I were building a traditional business?' The answer, in most cases, will be 'no'.

In the operation of a business there are a number of universal laws that apply to most enterprises. Whether a business is large or small, some aspects never change—for example, cash flow, communication, establishing systems, marketing, time management, etc. Network marketing is a business, and some of these universal laws will apply simply because you are in business.

One of the challenges often faced by those new to network marketing, especially those who have never been involved in their own business before, is the mistaken belief that these issues are unique to network marketing when they are first confronted with them. But if for this reason they choose to discontinue the business and move on to something else, they will find that the same issues still apply.

There was the case of Matthew, who had worked for someone else all his life but had always wanted a business of his own. On becoming aware of a network marketing opportunity he saw it as his chance, and decided to get involved. Soon he was confronted with some of the realities of running a business.

Because Matthew had never been in business before, he thought that some of the challenges he was facing were specific to his network marketing business and soon bailed out, commenting that 'network marketing does not work because it's just too hard'.

Sometime later, Matthew started a traditional business, where he was soon confronted with the same challenges. Unfortunately, he found those challenges also 'too hard', and this business failed too.

To help you better understand business generally, buy some books, do some small business courses, and mix with other business people, not just network marketing people. The more you can learn about business in general, the greater your chances of success in your network marketing business.

Network Marketing is a Numbers Game

The dream of all businesses is to have as many customers as possible buying their products or services, ideally 100 per cent of the total market. The reality is that all business owners recognize that they will only attract a certain amount of the market, or market share. In fact, larger organizations understand this principle so well that a large portion of their business planning is based around calculating how the numbers stack up. Based on experience and extensive research, most successful businesses know the percentages when it comes to market acceptance and market share. Whether it is a sole-trader bricklayer submitting a quote on a small retaining wall, or a multi-national engineering company submitting a tender on a major project, both understand that they are not going to win all quotes or tenders submitted. They realize it's a numbers game and that if they persist and keep submitting, they will win enough to be profitable.

Interestingly enough, the percentage conversion rate actually tells you a lot more. If you win every job you quote for, you are probably too cheap. If you get none, you are probably too expensive. The aim is to figure out what your conversion rate actually is. If you win five out of ten quotes and you want to build your business, submit more quotes. Simple as that.

As you build your network marketing business, for you the numbers game will mean finding those in the marketplace who may want to be involved and join your team, or those who wish to buy product from you. There will be those who do and those who don't. You can be sure of one thing, though— there will always be those that do. It simply means you have to persist, going through those that don't, to find the ones who do.

The bottom line is that doing business is a numbers game, and the more you work the numbers the better chance you have of winning the game. Your network marketing business is no different—not that you treat people like numbers, but if you can understand right from the word go that not everyone is going to want what you have to offer, even though you may think they should, this will make your journey so much easier.
If you work the numbers, the numbers will work for you.

You may not like everything about your business
As exciting as the opportunity is, the reality is that you may not like everything about your business or some of the things you are required to do to make it work. In a perfect world this wouldn't be the case, but we need to remember that there are probably things we don't like doing in our current traditional business or job—but we continue to do them because we understand that they are the price we pay to achieve the end result.

There is an interesting phenomenon which we call 'business envy'. It's that 'thing' which makes everyone else's business look so much better than our own. They look easier to run and far more profitable, cause fewer headaches, attract heaps of customers, and so on. In reality, we have yet to come across any business that is easy. Business envy needs to be kept well and truly in check.

There will be times when certain aspects of building your business will challenge you and put you outside your comfort zone. There will be things you simply do not like doing, find uncomfortable or don't agree with. It is vitally important that as you build your network marketing business you recognize this fact: 'Yes, there are certain things that I don't like doing and find challenging—but this is no different to the dislikes and challenges I found in what I was doing prior to my involvement in network marketing. But the price to pay for the end result is insignificant compared to the price I had to pay previously.'

We recommend that when you are feeling flat about your business you take the time to write down the positive aspects that really do make it feel worthwhile—the flexibility, the freedom, the creativity and the satisfaction gained from getting results. Focus on these positives and the negatives will soon seem less overwhelming.

Manage your Time, and Profitability
Because building a network marketing business is usually done part-time alongside what is more than likely an already busy schedule of work and family commitments, it is important to practice good time management. This, of course, will be easier for people who are well-organized by nature than for those who struggle to remember just which day it is.

Whatever your style, one thing is certain—to make a success of your network marketing business you will have to be organized and manage your time as effectively as possible. We all have 168 hours in a week. Why do some people seem to achieve so much more in their 168 hours than others? Usually it is because they maximize their time by managing it better.

Fortunately, good time management is not a difficult thing to achieve. For the most part it is driven by being organized and working from a diary. If you don't have a diary or have never worked from one, now is the time to start. There are many great books available on time management to assist those who struggle in this area. You might find that friends or business associates are willing to share their secrets and tips on how they manage to get so much done in a day. Time management is a skill that comes naturally to some but not to all. If your skills are lacking, do something about it.

Having your Door Open for Business
If you were establishing a traditional business and opened your doors to customers only a couple of days a week or your hours were inconsistent, how successful would you expect that business to be? Having your doors open for business is presenting your business to others or selling some product, yet many people go about their network marketing business doing very little of either and then question why it isn't working for them.
People who spend a lot of time thinking about the business or attending a lot of support training and seminars are often under the misapprehension that they are busy building the business, but in reality they are not keeping their doors open long enough to make their business work.

Here is a perfect real-life example of this attitude. David and Di, who were building a network marketing business, were meeting with Ian, their up-line coach, frustrated by their lack of results to date. They told Ian how excited they were about the opportunity and how they thought about it constantly, how they were reading and listening to as much support and motivational material as they could get their hands on, and were attending all the business meetings, seminars and functions that were being promoted to them. With all of this going on, in their minds they were busy building their business. But when Ian worked back through David and Di's diary over the last couple of months, they realized that the time they'd spent actually presenting the opportunity to others (building the business) was minimal, that the poor growth of their business was in direct relation to how often they'd had their doors open for business over that time. Once David and Di recognized the imbalance and addressed it, their business took off.

Taking time to think about and prepare plans for your business is important, and attending training and seminars is also a key ingredient, but if you want your business to grow quickly, do a regular reality check of your time to ensure that these elements are being equally matched by 'having your doors open for business'. You need to put out your 'NOW OPEN' sign every day to get customers walking in that door.

Set up a Separate Bank Account
It is important to set up a separate bank account to operate your network marketing business. If you were running a traditional business you would not attempt to operate the banking for it out of your personal account; the same applies here. Even though in the early days it may seem your business
is not big enough to warrant a separate bank account, you are laying the foundations of good business practice by starting off with a separate account straightaway.

Further to this, there will be expenses as you begin to build your business, many of them tax deductible. The costs associated with such expenses are far easier to monitor if the transactions are on a separate account. It can be difficult trying to identify them when they are mixed into your personal account.

All your network marketing expenses should be paid out of your business account, and any income derived should also be paid directly into that account. Don't make the mistake of paying any income from your network marketing business directly into your personal account while paying for expenses out of the business account, especially in the early days; otherwise it will seem that you are always spending money and never making any. Operating a separate account also allows for simpler accounting, which leads to easier assessment of income and expenses and the submitting of tax returns.

Another excellent reason for opening a separate bank account is simply that there is nothing quite as motivational as watching that account start to grow. As the balance increases, so does your energy and conviction. If the money coming in is somehow lost in the cracks there is little motivation to keep working on it. We play funny games in our minds, and a simple trick like this can have more impact than just about anything else.

Manage your money wisely

When operating any business it is critical to have in place some good accounting practices and a basic knowledge of bookkeeping. You don't need to rush off and get a degree in accounting—that's what your accountant is for—but it is important that you respect the need to keep good records and be organized. In the beginning you may feel there is no real need to pay too much attention to this area, but remember, you are laying the foundations for a much larger business.

More importantly, you are building a network of people who will look to you as an example and who will seek out advice on how to best build their businesses. If you do things correctly from the beginning, you will not have to go back and clean up the mess later.

It is often said in business that 'you can't manage if you can't measure'. Practicing good accounting will allow you to better measure where your business is financially and thus allow you to better manage it. Additionally, the way you structure your business while building it can have an effect on its profitability; good accounting practices will allow you to identify problems a lot more quickly and act to solve them.

If you have never been in business before, make an appointment with an accountant and get some advice on how to best set up your record keeping and books in general. Be aware that not all accountants will understand network marketing or be that positive towards it, largely because they've seen other clients not making a success of it.

If you are serious about your long-term network marketing career, you may want to sound out your accountant on their knowledge and support. If you feel he or she is lacking in these areas you might want to consider changing to one who is knowledgeable in the field, and supportive. Where a network marketing business is a supplementary source of income, and being run from home, there may be some considerable tax advantages and benefits, and possibly some pitfalls that you need to be aware of.

Getting the right advice will prove invaluable to maximize opportunity and to reduce risk.

Likewise, when you are starting to generate an income stream that is growing into a healthy monthly figure, you might want to consider how to best use this money. Some people use it as their annual holiday money, ensuring that they have a great overseas trip every year; others use it to fund a deposit on a new investment property every year. Then, of course, there are some who simply blow it, never taking full advantage of what the extra income could do for them and their future. What you do with the money you make from your network marketing business is entirely up to you, but we would recommend that you have some plans in place and ideally visit a good financial planner who can give you some professional advice along the way.

Chapter 6
Start Your Network Marketing Business Today

Network marketing's business model is simply leveraging the power of one-to-one relationships to market and distribute products directly to consumers. Network Marketing companies empower independent entrepreneurs to monetize the most viral form of marketing, which is word-of-mouth marketing. A network marketing professional is someone who leverages his or her social and professional relationships to market, sell and distribute products or services. At the same time, he or she will also be building a team of others who do the same.

"It's a pyramid, where the person at the top makes all the money." A good network marketing company rewards leadership, just like any structured business. Most businesses have a pyramid structure where the people at the top, ie. CEOs, SVPs, VPs, are the highest paid people in the company. The unique opportunity you have with a Network Marketing business is that you START at the top of your business, and your income will be dependent on how large of a team you build "below" you.

"You have to join a ground floor company to make the money." This is a perpetuated myth used by network marketers who build influence, and jump from company to company, and leverage this myth to recruit people from other Network Marketing companies. No network marketing company has ever "saturated" a market; it's just a perception of "saturation," not a reality.

"You have to know a lot of people, or be really good at sales to be successful."

Many good network marketing companies provide a system and training, so regardless of the size of your network – or ability to sell, you can be successful. Everything else is a learnable skill, and you have an abundance of people to practice networking with.

The Top Three Principles to Build a Successful MLM Business

You need to focus on helping others to get what they want, and you will get what you want. And remember, everything will rise and fall on LEADERSHIP.

- **First:** Invite people to look at your business proposition with a direct or indirect approach. A direct approach would be to ask them to look at your business for themselves. An indirect approach is asking someone to look at your business to assist you with recommendations or referrals. There are many different patterns of language that you can use based on the relationship you have with the prospective recruit. The invitation process is a very important skill to learn. Your invitation has a lot to do with whether the person will join your team or support your business.

- **Second:** Most people do not join on the first exposure, so fortune lies in the follow-up process. You must help to advance the prospective recruits understanding of your business on each follow-up interaction. Focus on building a stronger rapport and relationship along the way.

- **Third:** Use third-party social proof to validate the opportunity and to increase the prospect's belief that someone like them can be successful with your company.

- **Fourth:** Do a game plan interview and get the person off to a fast start. How you start a new person has a lot to do with their commitment level and how long they will build the business.

Because network marketing is a voluntary business, the retention of distributors is an important skill to learn.

- **Fifth:** Create a winning environment for your team to grow and for them to feed off the energy and excitement of others.

Of course the company needs to have a product that creates a valid demand in the marketplace. If that's the case, you leverage your network, and networks of others, to gain an audience of one or more. Share the benefits of your products or services, and share stories. Stories sell and facts tell.

In most cases, an indirect approach is best for friends and family. Ask them to support your business and vision by simply committing to take a good look at what you are doing and why you are doing it. Make it easy for them to say no and remain your friend. Don't pressure anyone.

Don't become weird. People join some network marketing businesses and get so excited that they don't separate their business from their personal lives. Don't redirect every conversation with your friends to try to recruit them into your business and don't turn your social media pages into an advertising bulletin board.

The key is to work by a calendar. Plan the times you will work your business. Most Network Marketing companies have tools and events system that allow you to leverage your time by promoting the SYSTEM to do the heavily lifting.

It's important to revisit the reasons why you started the business. It's also important to commit to personal development by listening and reading inspiring audios and books. Most people feel down because of the negative thoughts of self-doubt that start to creep into their minds.

I think a lot of people miss exactly how important it is to create a winning environment for your team to grow in. Ordinary people can win in an extraordinary environment.

The most useful skills need to use to achieve the best results in your businesses

- **Influence** – A leadership is influence, nothing more and nothing less. Everything rises and falls on leaderships, so it's an essential attribute for success. Influence is also used to effectively and persuasively communicate the virtues of a good product or service, and to get people to say YES! We also know that at sales.

- **Skills** – There are certain technical skills you need for whatever industry you are a part of, so it's important to develop those skills. Although, they are a small fraction of what your success will be predicated on. You must eventually learn to outsource the things that make the most sense to outsource, so that you can work on the business versus in the business.

- **Focus** – In today's fast paced society, the ability to focus is becoming a rarity. People are all over the place, and easily distracted. Time management is a myth, because time is already well managed into 24 hours a day. FOCUS Management is the challenge for us all. How to stay FOCUSED, and WHAT to focus on is also a topic in itself. It helps to have mentorship to assist you in this category.

- **Work Ethic** – The only place success comes before work is in the dictionary. It's important to build up your tolerance for work. If you are doing what you love, you work can become your play.

- **Belief** – As an entrepreneur, you are a creator. You turn intangible ideas into something tangible, and it requires belief! Not only does belief affect your physiology, but it also has an atmospheric affect that makes the universe start to conspire to that which you believe.

- **Faith** – The good book says, "Faith is the substance of things hoped for, and the evidence of things not seen." It requires faith to keep working when the results are not immediate. Entrepreneurship requires faith – the faith to believe even when it seems like believing is not working.

More Profitable in Your Network Marketing Business

Everyone wants to be more profitable. After all, profit is how we keep score in business. It's not about what you make – it is all about what you keep. Sometimes the simplest ideas can help you increase your profits. If you're ready to jumpstart the money making activities in your enterprise, implement these effective ways to be more profitable in your network marketing business!

"   Go through customer files. They are a gold mine.

How many customers are in your database? How many customers are active customers (you've done business with them in the past 18 months)? Usually the number of customers in the file is much greater, sometimes exponentially greater, than the number of active customers.

Reactivate your inactive customers. Send a postcard series with the theme "We want you back." You'll be surprised at how many call and say, "We thought you went out of business since we hadn't heard from you in a long time."

These people have purchased from you at least once. Give them a reason to purchase from you again!

"   Know your net profit per hour.

Net profit per hour is total net profit before taxes divided by billable hours or revenue producing hours. Include all employee hours from all employees it took to deliver your products and services. Do not include training hours, vacation hours, etc.

It says for every hour that you produce revenue, what is the bottom line profit that you generate? If the number is lower than you'd like, then take steps to increase it. This might be raising prices, adding additional products and services to increase the total sale to one customer, increasing employee productivity, or cutting overhead. Ask your employees how to decrease costs or increase sales by $100 per month. They can relate to $100 and probably will have some great ideas. Implement them and they will continue to give you great ideas.

"   Don't get stupid when you get busy.

Discipline in busy times as you discipline in slower times. When it is busy you have a tendency to let infractions "slip under the rug" because you don't make the time to deal with them. The fear is that you can't afford to be without that person because it is busy. If an employee does a fire able offense, he must be fired. It doesn't matter what time of year it is.

If you don't fire that person, your revenues may start to slip. Other employees will see that "someone got away with something" and they will be less likely to work as hard. Less hard work means less revenue. Less revenue usually means less profit.

" Ask for referrals.

One of the best ways to grow your company is through referrals from happy customers. Put a statement at the bottom of your invoices, on proposals, and the back of your business cards.

Print "We grow our company through referrals from satisfied customers. If we provided excellent products and customer service, please tell your friends and colleagues. If we did something wrong, please tell us and we will fix it. Our goal is 100% customer satisfaction."

This statement lets a customer know that you are serious about providing outstanding customer service and that you appreciate referrals. Some will call you with referrals. Some will let you fix a problem rather than spreading the fact that they were unhappy to friends, neighbors, and social media.

" Call 30 days after you make the sale.

The person who sold the product/project or a customer service representative should call 30 days after the sale to make sure that everything is ok. He should ask for referrals by asking,
"Who have you talked to about your new _____?"
When the customer answers he says, "Do you think NAME would be as happy as you are with a new _____ like you have?"
When the customer says. "Ask NAME." Get NAME's contact information and follow up on this referral.

" Save 1% of every dollar that comes in the door.

This is your emergency cash account. For each bank deposit, write a check or transfer 1% of that deposit amount into a savings account when you make the deposit. You still have 99% to use. That 1% will be there when you need cash for payroll or taxes.

Get timely, accurate financial statements each month.
Reviewing these statements takes less than 30 minutes per month. You will spot minor issues and can take care of them before they become major crises. You will also be able to make great business decisions based on the accurate information you get.

Implement these simple ideas. They can help you generate more profit today in your small business.

How to Attract Customers to Your Network Marketing Business

When it comes to doing business these days, the deal is – no one wants to be sold to. You must give consistently to eventually get business, especially if you are a professional service business. Here are my 7 ways to attract customers to a small business

1. **It's all about service**. You must first try to be helpful when building relationships with prospective clients. It's all about providing valuable content, engaging people to build a relationship, being a good listener and making sure you are a trusted resource before you attempt to sell anything.

2. **Understand Your Business First:** What do you do and how does it serve your customer? What is your (UVP), Unique Value Proposition? How do you serve your customers and solve their problems?

3. **Focus On a Specific Customer** Develop a detailed customer profile. Who is your customer? How does she live? Is she married with children or a single working professional? Is she a Baby Boomer or Millennial? Create a mental image of her, and make sure your marketing messages and content speak specifically to her. Remember – if everybody can use your product or service, no one will!

4. **Attract Your Niche Customer** Depending on who your customer is, some marketing methods will work better than others. Once you develop your customer profile, figure out how to reach them specifically. The more niche focused your business is in the marketplace, the easier it is to reach your market. Start by

developing a list of your top 4-6 keywords. These are the top search terms people use to find your products and services online.

5. **Determine Your Marketing Approach** Your marketing approach will be determined by your niche target customer. Try a few of these ideas to reach your target customer.

- Develop a Great Website
- Content marketing/Blogging
- Email marketing
- Pay per click ads
- Direct mail
- Vehicle wrap
- Flyers/ billboards
- Newspapers/magazines

6. Create a Referral Machine Turn your happy customers into an unpaid sales force for your business. Incentivize your customers with discounts and special sales to tell their friends about your business. Find unique ways to reward and acknowledge your most loyal customers. Host a customer appreciation event or give a social media shout out to your customers. Everyone loves acknowledgement.

7. Keep Your Customers It's cheaper to keep a customer than to go chase a new one. Your best opportunity to generate more revenue is to upsell an existing customer. The best way to upsell customers is to keep in touch with them. Here are a few ideas to incorporate into your business.

- Contact customers within 7-10 days of a sale
- Conduct an online survey about your customer service
- Invite customers to leave a review on your website, LinkedIn, Yelp, Angie's list, TripAdvisor, Google+ local, or Yahoo local listings
- Send an email newsletter at least monthly (weekly is best)
- Send birthday cards
- Send holiday cards (It's not just about Xmas, try Valentine's Day or 4th of July cards, too)
- Ask for feedback on Facebook and Twitter

If you start using these methods of marketing and sales in your business, you will see more repeat customers and that means your business will become sustainable. Remember anyone will buy something once; you need to build a relationship to get them to buy it over and over again from you.

Hey if you need more help with sales, if have an amazing free resource for you. One of my favorite sales experts Jeffrey Gitomer and I are giving you a free, five-part webinar series called, "How to Really Make Sales." You know Jeffrey from his New York Times Bestseller, "The Little Red Book of Selling." Jeffrey is a master at sales and I know you'll benefit greatly from our knowledge and advice during the "How to Really Make Sales" five-part webinar series.

Chapter 7
Winning Strategy for Your Network Marketing Business

In the excitement to launch a potentially lucrative business, the temptation is to take a "fire, ready, aim!" approach and dive right in. But if you don't take a good look first and account for what lies below the surface, you could be setting yourself up for a painful experience.

One of the wonderful things about network marketing is that the most important factor in the success equation is the person running the business— you. You don't need a lot of money or fancy office space or great connections to make a go of it. What you do need, however, is a plan that enables you to make the most of the resources in your possession.

There is no magic formula or instructions carved in stone for putting together a strategy. The major task of a strategy, however, is to establish a clear purpose and direction for your business. In this chapter we will learn about the nine key tasks that need to be completed in order to construct and customize your own strategy. The nine key tasks fall into nine areas and are:

1) **Life priorities.** Clearly state the priorities that are important to you as you look to the future.

2) **Purpose.** Clearly state your reasons for building the business, your overall purpose, and what you are striving to achieve.

3) **Vision. Create a vision** of what you want your future to be and communicate it to everyone associated with your business.

4) **Core values.** Identify your core values and use them to drive behavior and as the criteria for decision making.

5) **Core skills.** Identify your core skills and the skills that are required for success. Leverage these skills to establish competitive advantage in the marketplace.

6) **Marketplace.** Examine the marketplace in which you operate, determine the threats and opportunities, and then select target markets to capitalize on. Be clear about how you intend to penetrate your chosen markets.

7) **System.** Ensure the provision of a system that meets the needs of your team in the markets where you will be required to support the implementation of your business strategy.

8) **Key interfaces.** Identify key internal and external interfaces, assess their impact on your business, and develop effective strategies to determine and address their needs and interests.

9) **Key resources.** Identify the tangible and intangible resources that are key to your business, and ensure an adequate supply of them.

Individuals vary in how far along they are in the development of the key areas. Most of us like to focus on what we're best at and maybe take care of the rest as we go along. We should, in fact, pay the closest attention to the areas where we are weakest; for it is here that our strategy is in the most danger of coming apart.

Most Critical Skill Every Network Marketer Professional Must Possess

Many people would say that recruiting is the most important skill in network marketing. Others would say contacting and inviting. Even more would argue it's learning to be effective on the phone. I disagree with all of these answers. All are important, but not most important. Before any of these skills contribute to building your network marketing empire, you're going to have to be mentally tough. In other words, you're going to have to learn to become a master of your emotions. This means learning how to control your thoughts, feelings, and attitudes— especially under pressure.

Why is this single most critical skill? Because without it you will fail. Period. The rejection you face on a daily basis in this business will wipe you out, just as it has wiped out millions of other sharp, ambitious, well-educated people. The masses don't understand network marketing, and their ignorance often takes the form of ridicule. If you are mentally tough enough to keep bouncing back while growing stronger with each attack, you have a legitimate shot at living your dream in this business. There are no guarantees, but you have a shot.

The majority of people are addicted to the approval of others. Most of us are taught from an early age to place a high value on what other people think of us. We're told to obey the rules, respect our elders, and comply with society's value structure. When we stray from these commands, we are punished. Network marketing demands that you abandon this philosophy and dive into the mix. In other words, make a decision to place your highest value on your approval of yourself. This is a decision to lead rather than follow.

The Gallup Organization tells us there are approximately 10 million leaders in the world leading approximately 6 billion people. Your ability to break any addiction you might have to acquiring the approval of others will determine which group you fall into.

The masses are not engaged in critical thinking. The average prospect you're contacting is more concerned about what television program they're going to watch tonight than they are about securing their future. By middle age, most people have given up hope of converting their dreams into reality and subsequently seek solace in activities where effort is minimal and pleasure is king. According to USA Today, the average American watches 1,669 hours of television per year. My point is that the average person's criticism of your opportunity shouldn't carry much weight if you're a true leader. I'm not putting anyone down; I'm simply suggesting the next time you experience a harsh rejection to consider the source. On the other end of the spectrum, most successful people are slow to ridicule something they don't understand.

These people are accustomed to using their critical thinking skills on a daily basis and tend to carefully consider and weigh all options before reaching a conclusion.

How mentally tough are you? Mental toughness means controlling your emotions in performance situations, and people who are mentally tough develop thick skin when it comes to rejection. Mental toughness in network marketing is developed by getting in front of a predetermined number of prospects every day, either on the phone or face-to-face. The people who join you won't make you mentally tough. The people who decline but are positive about the business won't make you tough, either. It's the people that laugh at you and the whole concept of network marketing that will temper the steel inside your psyche. They will facilitate your emotional growth or they will blow you out of the business. It depends on how tough you are when the rejection hits.

The secret to survival is mental preparation. Many of the network marketing leaders I've encountered over the past 20 years spend a substantial amount of time trying to persuade their prospects and distributors how easy it is to build a successful network marketing business, while behind the scenes working 12-to-15-hour days. The average leader in this profession spends a lot of time trying to control attrition and sponsor new people.

The yearly attrition rate in network marketing is well over 90 percent, and the reason is lack of mental preparation. Instead of telling people how easy it is to build a million-dollar business, do the direct opposite. Tell them it's going to be difficult.

Prepare them for the onslaught of rejection headed their way. Give them examples. Role-play with them. Let them experience the emotional assault that awaits them in the field. This doesn't guarantee their success, but it gives them a fighting chance to survive their first year in the business.

Take a tip from trial lawyers. Go for the throat during role-play. If you've ever observed a trial lawyer preparing a client or witness to be cross-examined, you have the blueprint to effective role-play for mental toughness. The lawyer's job is to simulate the attack the client is about to encounter, especially during emotionally charged questions and accusations. The goal is to get under the client's skin and tap the anger, frustration, and guilt before the opposing lawyer has a chance to do the same thing in court in front of the jury. At first, the witness is shocked by the attack. But after a while he becomes desensitized to the emotionally charged language and begins to emotionally separate himself.

Spaced repetition is the secret. The emotional toughening process works best through spaced repetition. I would recommend at least four training sessions in the first 30 days after the new distributor signs up. The key is to keep him or her out of the field before this training is completed. The old strategy of throwing a new person out in the field before arming him or her with the mental tools necessary to survive is unfair at best, and malpractice at worst.
Your job as a leader is to help prepare your charge for what lies ahead on the battlefield. Be responsible and do it right. Competent coaching means investing the necessary time to do the job properly.

Start with the premise of the problem. Excited new network marketers can't understand why the entire world doesn't get it. They often go out in the field for the first time with the expectation that everyone is going to see the opportunity like they do. When people don't respond, they are incredulous. It just doesn't make sense to them. They were so sure everyone would see it the way they do. Your job as a leader/coach is to help them accept the fact that most people ridicule network marketing because they don't understand it.
The average person is intelligent enough but mentally unengaged, and to fully comprehend the magnitude of opportunity that network marketing presents you have to study it. Most people would rather go to happy hour or watch a ball game than seriously consider your company's compensation plan. This is not an insult. It's a statistical fact. If the average person really understood network marketing, chances are they would get involved. It's ingenious, and anyone who understands the principles of marketing and distribution will see that. Once your new person understands that the laughter and ridicule they experience say more about the prospect than about the profession, they have a mental foundation to work from.

Next, prepare them for the five major objections. Survey the most active distributors in your company and ask them to list the five most common objections they encounter in the field. Next, ask them to give you their best response to these objections. Once you have this information, role-

play with your new people until they can recite the proper responses by heart. They aren't fully prepared until they can repeat the responses quickly and naturally.
This takes time and patience, and it's a critical part of their mental training.
Once they get good, get tougher in the role-play. Change the words of the objections around and try to throw them off. Then reverse roles and let them play the prospect. This gives them a chance to see their mentor in action. You had better be prepared, and you'd better be good. I can promise you that any successful trial lawyer could take the witness stand and endure the emotional assault of the best prosecutor in the world. If you're a true leader you'll be able to do the same. Put in the same practice time you're asking your new distributor to invest. If you don't, you can be sure you will get caught. Once you do, your credibility is gone.

Finally, explain the brain's primary purpose. To cap off this introductory phase of mental toughness training, explain to people how their brain works. The brain's primary purpose is to preserve and protect the mind and body. When an event occurs, the brain asks three questions: (1) what is it? (2)
What does it mean? (3) What do I do?

Let's say the event is a prospect rejecting the new distributor. The average person has been conditioned to interpret rejection as a negative, and even psychologically threatening, event. As a result, they respond defensively and sometimes aggressively. The rejection itself is not the problem. The real menace is in the meaning that the distributor has assigned to it. The good news is that the meaning of an event is only a perception, and perceptions can be altered through reprogramming. The significance is that if you change what rejection means, you automatically change the response to it. Train your people to interpret every rejection as being one step closer to sponsoring the next person. Train them to understand that rejection is what accounts for the big money that is paid out to top distributors in this profession. Have you ever heard of a retail salesperson making a million dollars a year? No, because the rejection factor is low and the customer comes to them, so more people can do it successfully. It's simply not worth that much in the marketplace because so many people can do it. It's all supply and demand. Once they understand that rejection creates the barrier of entry for 99 percent of network marketers to become successful, they will get excited to know they are among the top 1 percent. Let them know they are part of an elite group of people in the profession who understand how the business really works. You will have to program them to believe this by emphasizing it over and over until they're mentally tough enough to stand on their own.

Get help with the programming process. As leader and coach to your organization, it's your responsibility to shape and mold your people into competent network marketing professionals. That being said, you can't do it all.

You can get them started and encourage them along the way, but you're going to need help. Train your people to invest in books, CDs, and seminars on topics like mental toughness, motivation, and vision building—anything that keeps world-class ideas in front of them when you're not there. Remember they are surrounded, as we all are, by middle-class thinkers. Consciousness is contagious, so be sure they are exposed to the best of the best. Ninety days of this type of programming and exposure should be enough to enable them to stand on their own. If they are still dependent on you after that, move on and invest your precious time in someone else. Everyone has the ability to access their mental toughness, but many choose (consciously or unconsciously) not to tap into it. In a profession where momentum is critical to your success, you don't have time to wait for the slow movers. Make a commitment today. Decide that you will become a mental toughness expert to ensure your success. Begin with these simple steps, and you'll be well on your way.

Chapter 8
The Building Real Residual Income to your Network Marketing Business

There is something very special about most legitimate network marketing opportunities. It is not always obvious and not always fully appreciated for what it is and what it can mean to most families. Behind all of the excitement and expectations of newfound financial freedom is the real essence of what financial security is all about. Clearly, it is very important for the new prospect or seasoned networker to look beyond the promise of huge up-front money—the $10,000 per month in 90 days to $1 million or more per month as you build your business. While this possibility can be real in many cases, it is more elusive for most.

When all of the dust has settled and the initial excitement has faded, what really matters in terms of wealth generation is how much money you are receiving each month—today—for the work that you did yesterday. That is residual income. I believe that most of us would easily opt for $10,000 per month for the rest of our lives (and our survivors') rather than $50,000 per month for a few months. When we combine the concept of residual income with that of leverage, we are indeed on our way to permanent financial security.

I invite you to read this chapter not only from the perspective of how residual income can impact your life but how you can use the value of residual income to attract your prospects to your networking business.

Let's take a step back to look at the very special financial perspective of network marketing. First, allow me to provide a little background. I have been a financial planner since 1968 and a Certified Financial Planner (CFP) since 1978. During this time, I have spent endless hours with clients trying to help structure retirement plans and to help establish financial security. It has seemed that no matter how hard most people try, they have either too little time or too little money. There are, after all, not many ways to accumulate significant wealth. You need to have either sufficient fund to make the most of your limited time to accumulate or a lot of time during which to build you're the young, who have the time in which to accumulate, rarely have the discipline to do it. The older folks, who have the burning, need and some limited resources, just do not usually have the time left to reach their goal.

It has become clearer every day that just working at a job is not the answer.
The old idea of working 40 years on the job and retiring with a gold watch just does not work today. We are living longer, working harder, and making less, and have even less to show for our efforts. Nine out of 10 families now need two working members just to make ends meet. Surveys also indicate that 85 percent of all Americans would like to own their own business.
With that in mind, let's look at how many people are effectively addressing the problem.

In the United States, someone starts a new home-based business every 10 seconds. More than 25 percent of all Americans are involved in some sort of home business, and the numbers are even more dramatic in other parts of the world. The average successful home-based business generates more than $50,000 yearly in income, while the average working wage is only $22,000 in North America. The reason for the great disparity, to a great extent, is due to the concepts of residual income and leverage. We will touch briefly on leverage here and get into a more detailed discussion of residual income shortly.

The concept of leverage was most clearly stated by J. Paul Getty, the oil industry billionaire, who said, "I'd rather have 1 percent of 100 people's efforts than 100 percent of my own." It would be hard to state this principle any more clearly or have it make any more sense. Since network marketing is all about word-of-mouth communications with others, it epitomizes the principle of leverage. You tell someone something that you feel strongly and passionately about, and they tell someone, who tells someone, who tells someone.

And so it goes. Before you know it, you have an organization building your business while they are building their own. Remember, most people are involved in network marketing now; they just aren't getting paid for it. Isn't that what happens when one recommends a restaurant, movie, or product?

How much would you have made if you got a check every time you made a recommendation? Well, you can with network marketing.

I became deeply involved with network marketing about 25 years ago when I was doing some research for a financial planning client. He was about 60 years old and was about to leave a job that he had been at for more than 30 years. His company retirement plan was to give him an income for life of about 50 percent of the salary that he barely survived on while working—not a very promising prospect. At his request, I looked into several network marketing opportunities and discovered something incredible from a financial planning perspective. That was, it seemed reasonable to assume that within two to four years in network marketing, my client could build a residual income that could equal or exceed his retirement income, and this income could continue to grow and pay not only him, but his heirs upon his death. What a financial planning tool!

Let's put a pen to this and utilize some financial planning concepts to put the picture into its proper perspective. Let's look at the concept of asset equivalency. What would be the equivalent cash asset needed to replace a reliable, continuing cash flow generated as a result of residual income from a network marketing enterprise? First of all, we must accept the premise that this type of residual income can be stated as if it were the return on a cash asset. For our illustration, we are going to assume a very safe investment equivalent: a bank certificate of deposit or (CD), in this case, one that yields a better than average return of 3 percent. Treat the following illustration in this manner: A benefactor has given you a lump sum of money and has required that it be placed in a CD. This enables you to receive the income for life and your heirs will continue to do so thereafter, provided you do not touch the principal.

Let's assume you have joined a network marketing company that offers a true residual income opportunity. You have studied well and worked hard. It is now one year into the effort and you have built a $2,500 per month residual income. From a planning view, you have created a personal asset possessing a net worth of $1 million. Assuming a 3 percent yield on your money, 3 percent of $1 million equals $30,000 per year, or $2,500 per month. Yes, you are now a millionaire!

But you are not ready to quit yet. Let's see what can happen with a bit more effort if you continue to do exactly what you were doing that got you to where you are. You are working and getting others to work in a compensation plan that has rewarded you with this income. Over the next 12 months, you do not work any harder and you do not work any smarter, but at the end of this time your monthly residual income is now $5,000 per month. That's right, you now have the equivalent of $2 million in the bank, and are earning as if your $2 million was generating 3 percent.

I think that you have the picture. Without working harder or smarter, each year you're net worth increases by $1 million and your income by $30,000. You may decide to work harder or smarter, but it is also acceptable to go and spend your remaining days on the beach, as long as you have developed leaders who will continue to support their organizations. Your income should continue to grow, as will your net worth. One of the beautiful aspects of this scenario is the benefit that your heirs will receive upon your death. The income should continue and pass on to your heirs without serious erosion from the effects of estate or inheritance taxes.

There are a number of important factors to put into place to make sure that the income you have built is residual. Most network marketing businesses have the element of helping and caring for others. It is critical that you become a product of your products, that you truly care about what you are doing, that you support your customers ethically, and that you empower your distributors who themselves become leaders. Your rock-solid belief and the enthusiasm with which you present yourself and your opportunity will be the key to your success.

Let's step back a minute and examine where you are. You have now found the right company with the right business plan. You have examined the compensation plan and it works for you. Your family is supportive and you have a fire in your belly. It is now time to learn the business as well as you can and put what you learn to work. Plan your work and work your plan. Don't get discouraged because at some point along the way to success you will likely hit the wall. Keep on plugging, inspired by the reasons that had you join your company in the first place, and it will be well worth it in the long run. If you work your business with all of the energy that you can muster, you will achieve success and, as a result, life will never be the same.

Network marketing companies possess several key components that will ensure that the residual income created will last long into the future. Every element does not have to be present to the same degree in every program, but there is a relationship between the reliability of the income and the presence of the following elements:

- High demand.
- Great value.
- Limited competition.
- Affordable pricing.
- Continuous need.
- Ready availability.
- Geographic availability.
- Products or services backed by a guarantee or warranty

It is critical that once a customer or distributor has made the initial commitment to the product or service, the revenue is repeatable without effort.

What makes it work is that the benefits outweigh the costs, yielding the ability to keep on adding new customers and distributors without losing old ones.

Network marketing has traditionally been an eyeball-to-eyeball, belly-to-belly business. That method has worked for decades and will for decades to come, but in today's world of the Internet and electronic marketing, more and more people are finding success without stepping away from their telephone and computer. The best way is the way that works best for you. In a large organization, success will typically result from a combination of techniques, but never forgetting the basics of people-to people, relationship marketing.

As a network marketing millionaire, or budding millionaire, there are now other things for you to consider:

- What am I going to do with my money?
- How long and hard do I want to work?
- What is my definition of financial freedom?
- Who do I want to bring along with me?

These are not easy questions, but ones that you surely can answer. You will also have the opportunity to do some necessary financial planning and tax planning. As an independent business owner, you are entitled to hundreds of tax benefits that can amount to many thousands of dollars each and every year. The combination of residual income and self-employment tax benefits represents some of the most powerful financial tools anyone can access. You will soon understand why the rich and famous can stay rich and famous—or at least rich.

Here is your final challenge. Given the experience of working with hundreds and maybe thousands of network marketing millionaires, the ultimate challenge may not be how to become a millionaire, but what to do when you become a millionaire. Residual income millionaires may be faced with choices that they have never dealt with before in their lives—choices like:

- What time do I want to get up today?
- Do I want to work today?
- Where do I want to be today?
- What do I want to do today?
- How do I want to spend the rest of my life?

Network marketing can be a vehicle for doing as much good as possible for as many people as possible, and getting paid for doing it! There are people who have some very definite personal goals that can be attainable with the level of financial security made possible by a million-dollar residual income.

These might include:

- Gaining a long overdue education.
- Sending someone to college.
- Doing mission work or contributing to charity.
- Creating a new home for oneself or one's family.
- Having the means to afford all the material things that make life fun and exciting.

There is no right or wrong when it comes to making these choices since they are so personal. Financial freedom can certainly be a worthy goal for which to strive. How you obtain it and what you do with it are up to you. Network marketing can give you the best shot at joining the top 2 percent of earners in America. It is up to you to make it happen.

Chapter 9
Overcoming Challenges, Obstacles, and Fear

The first step in overcoming challenges, obstacles, and problems is to accept the fact that they are inevitable. It is naive to expect that something great will be easy.

For most of my life, in my arrogance and shortsightedness, I'd quickly get irritated at problems, thinking, "It is not supposed to be this way" or "This should not be happening." Now, most of the time I remember that things are not supposed to be smooth and easy—except in my unrealistic expectation of how the world is supposed to be.

The second step in overcoming challenges and obstacles is to take a point of view that they are a necessary and useful part of life—that they are actually good and working ultimately to my benefit. Without challenges, obstacles, and problems, we would remain soft and weak, and it is only because of them that we can become strong, creative, resourceful, and victorious. Lifting small easy weights will not develop my muscles to be stronger or bigger; but the bigger the weights, the bigger the muscles. The bigger the problem, challenge, or obstacle, the bigger and stronger I become.

The third step in overcoming challenges and obstacles is to have a heartfelt appreciation for them as my teachers and my coach. I can choose to see them accompanied by an invisible purpose of making me better, wiser, and stronger, and for that, I can be grateful. Rather than resenting, I can appreciate them. Just taking this point of view immediately empowers me. Plus, it positions me to get all the benefits from dealing with the inevitable challenges and obstacles that I have to deal with anyway (unless I succumb to resignation and give up).

But I will forfeit the not-so-obvious benefits if I go to my old way of thinking (paradigm) that "it is not supposed to be this way," that problems are bad and are simply deterrents to me getting what I want. Plus, there is little satisfaction in not having something to overcome, a battle to win, a giant to kill. The bigger the mountain, the greater the glory when I get to the top.

There is a part of us that needs to conquer and overcome.

The other huge benefit of having a problem that is bigger than you is that you are then forced to enroll others into working with you in order to create a solution. You get a partner. You find a coach. You learn how to build a team that will be far more powerful than you ever would have been by yourself. You leverage your weakness and inadequacy to upgrade yourself from a small life of just you to a bigger life of working with others as a team.

If instead of appreciation I go into resistance and resentment, I create at least two new problems. The first one is stress—we already have too much of that! This can damage my health and shorten my life, as well as rob me of the enjoyment of life. The second problem I create by being in resistance and resentment is the very resistance that I think will combat the problem actually hold it more strongly in place. What I resist persists.

If instead, I embrace the problem with appreciation, as an opportunity to grow and be creative, I will be empowered to deal with it more effectively and actually overcome it faster. Instead of unknowingly contributing to the problem's persistence by my resistance, I will also be creating a better me.

The fourth step in overcoming challenges and obstacles is discerning ahead of time what they are going to be. The most serious and dangerous ones are the ones we create ourselves. The external obstacles are actually easier to handle. The greatest enemy is within, which is fear or anticipation of pain.

WHAT ARE THEY THINKING OF ME
Your biggest and most serious obstacle to managing is your concern (anticipation of pain) as to what people think about you. As you share yourself, your ideas, your perspective, your goals, and your dreams with others, some of them will not support what you are saying or doing. There is a possibility that you could even be put down or ridiculed. Two thousand years ago when the Apostle Peter gave his first presentation, some were amazed, some were confused, some mocked, and some believed. The pattern is still true today.

This concern (anticipation of emotional pain) of what people think of you manifests internally as anxiety. Externally, it shows up as procrastination or not taking any action at all. If you are not fully aware of this, you will be ambushed by it, and not really know what hit you! It knocks many out of the game, and they never return. To be forewarned is to be forearmed.
However, don't have an unrealistic expectation that you can eliminate this universal concern—I don't think we can totally, and we don't need to.
The best most of us can do is manage it and not let it dominate us, and that is enough. Another challenge will be your disappointment that some people will is almost inevitable that you will get discouraged, and that is okay as long as you are not surprised by it, and you don't stay stuck there. Just acknowledge it, feel it, and dismiss it as you move on.
Another obstacle will be your own unrealistic expectations. These can set you up for yielding to the temptation of quitting. Usually, things do not go as smoothly or as quickly as you expect. The answer is to not drop your expectations because there is truth to the adage that you get what you expect. It just may take longer.

The way to be less affected is to not be emotionally attached to the results.
You can be 100 percent committed to creating a certain result, but if it doesn't happen as you expected, it does not mean that you are not good enough or that you were wrong. If you are emotionally attached to your results, you will take your lack of results personally and judge yourself as inadequate, or even worse, as stupid or worthless. You will take yourself

out of the game, and cheat yourself of the reward that comes from making a difference.
And others will be hurt as well by your giving up and quitting. By default, you create lose-lose instead of a win-win situation.

Set goals and have expectations that stretch you, but don't makeup something negative about yourself (i.e., disempower yourself) if it doesn't happen as fast as you expect. If you don't get what you want, what does that mean? It means you didn't get what you want. Anything else beyond that is your interpretation, which you are then in danger of using against yourself to disempower yourself.

Another obstacle or challenge is the many distractions that dilute your focus and get you off track. You must be aware of this and get yourself back on track and refocused as soon as you realize you are off. Pay attention, adjust, and advance—correct and continue.

The greatest enemy of the best is the good. Do not settle for something that is good when there is something else that is better or even the best. For example, doing paperwork, checking e-mail, reading, getting organized, and so on are all good and recommended activities. But if these good things displace more important things that actually move the action forward, then the better choice has lost out to the merely good, often as a way of avoidance.
Stay focused and remembers this: The main thing is to keep the main thing the main thing! The main thing is the mission of making a difference.
Another major obstacle is one we create—our sense of inadequacy and lack of confidence. This can be the most disempowering and disabling challenge.
It is the number one reason most people don't even get into the game and is the main reason most people will do far less than they could have.

The good thing about feeling inadequate is that it can keep us from falling into a worse trap of arrogance and pride. It keeps us from becoming too independent and overconfident. But that does not matter—you can still succeed. Just do not let your lack of confidence keep you out of the game. The best way to handle feeling inadequate is to accept it as normal, to commit to being teachable and getting trained, and then to play to win. Have a partner, be part of a team, get coaching, and ask for help and feedback.

YOU HAVE THE POWER

Consider the source of fear and faith. Both have the same source: your imagination.

You generate or create either one. We tend to think that fear or faith comes from the outside, but actually, they do not even exist for you unless you create them. For example, consider the concept of fear of rejection. This is a huge obstacle for most people. This fear of rejection seems to be very real, and it paralyzes people. The real problem is not rejection. It is the fear of rejection. This fear of rejection is not something that happens to you—it is something you create. It is not real. Actually, all that is really happening is an anticipation of emotional pain, a belief that someone may judge you, which you interpret as painful.

Want to know how to overcome the fear of rejection? It's easy. Just face the truth. That's it. The truth is that there is very seldom any real rejection in life, even though there is a great deal of fear of rejection. Here's my evidence.

If I'm sharing an idea with you and you tell me that you are not interested, or that you think that my idea is stupid or crazy, or whatever, I may tell myself that I was just rejected.

Here's what actually happened:
- I told you what I believed.
- You told me your opinion.
- Your opinion was different from my opinion.
- I concluded that you rejected me.

So where is the rejection? All that really happened was that there was a difference of opinion. There was no rejection! If you said to me, "Ray, I reject you," now I've been rejected. But how often does that happen? Unless I am told directly, "I reject you," there is no rejection going on. The only "rejection "is what I imagined. With this, I disempower myself.

Well, someone may say, maybe the guy just didn't say it, but he was actually rejecting me. So let's check it out. If I ask you, "Are you rejecting me?" you are going to say, "No, I'm not rejecting you—I'm just rejecting what you said." But it doesn't even matter whether or not I am rejected because it is the fear that is the problem.

Even if you did reject me, so what? Am I damaged or injured? Will I die? But, if I can just see the truth that there is no rejection anyway, I have nothing to fear. I am anticipating pain that will never happen, like a little boy or girl who is anticipating the pain (getting hurt or killed) by the monster under the bed that does not even exist! The monster is merely an illusion (I recommend that you watch the movie James and the Giant Peach).

So, choose to create faith instead of creating fear. Like the angry mother said to her disobedient child—"I brought you into the world, and I can take you out!" Any fear that you have, you created. So, you can UN-create it by creating a faith that instantly displaces it. Choose an environment and people who are congruent with faith, which lives by faith. We are all susceptible to fear, and we can all become people of great faith. It's your choice. Make the choice that best serves you and that empowers you to live life fully.

FEAR MAKES YOU SMALL, WHILE FAITH MAKES YOU BIG

More precisely, the fear that you create so disempowers you that you believe the lie that you are small and incapable, or that you will not survive some pain that might happen. Fear has a contracting effect and creates a self-generated prison. Even though it is an illusion, at the time you do not realize that it is an illusion because it seems so real. So you remain small and trapped. You feel like a helpless victim.

In contrast, faith and confidence empower you by helping you realize and accept the truth that you are, by design, powerful and capable, that you can survive any pain that might happen. Living by faith allows you to live life fully in an ever-expanding way. Isn't that what you want? Whereas fear has a contracting effect and creates a prison, faith expands you and frees you to enjoy the freedom that you have. You are a powerful being with the power to create. God creates—He is the ultimate creator. Made in His image, you also create, automatically. You have been creating your entire life, even though most of the time we create unconsciously, thinking that things just happen and that we are victims of circumstances.

So, as the creator you are, you can choose to create fear or you can choose to create faith. So, since it is your choice, why not create the faith that gives your life and freedom? Isn't that what you want? If you don't create faith, by default, you are probably creating fear that only rips you off, and ultimately it rips off others due to your inaction. Remember that just as darkness can exist only in the absence of light, fear can exist only in the absence of faith. Focus on creating faith, and fear will become a minor issue, as it is displaced by faith.

Think of what is at stake—your life, and the lives of others. Think of what it will cost you to allow yourself to be dominated by fear—the very fear you created. You cannot afford to pay this ungodly price of living by fear! So, make a conscious choice and commitment to create faith and live by faith, and you will overcome all obstacles, challenges, and fear itself. You were created to be a winner—so be a winner! Think and live as one and you will create winning.

TRUE SELF VERSUS FALSE SELF

The true you, the person you really are deep inside, are a person of faith and love, who believes in yourself and in the future. The real you are good, loving, and powerful. The real you live in faith and confidence. The result of living from the true self is happiness and creating a big life with a big impact in the world.

The false you, the imposter, are the person who is run by fear. The false self is weak and insecure. The result is a small life with a small impact. The key to living life fully is to remember who you really are, underneath the artificial layers of fear that have been self-created: a person of love and faith. Be that person—be the real you! Who you are is important, and by living out of faith you make a meaningful difference! I challenge and invite you to live life fully, free of fear and full of faith!

Important Questions to Ask Myself

- On a scale from 0 to 10, the number that best represents how well I handle my concern (fear) about how people may judge or disapprove of me is ____.

- On the same scale, the number that best represents my level of confidence, based on the past, present, and future, is ____.

- On the same scale, the number that best represents how well I handle the illusion of rejection is ____.

- On the same scale, the number that best represents my commitment to creating faith instead of creating fear is ____.

THE POWER OF ONE

One is a small number, but it can make a big difference. There is power in one. One makes a difference. The entire human population started with one. Oneness of mind (agreement and unity) makes a difference.

- How many points does it take to win or lose a game? What happens if you misdial a phone number by one digit? What happens if you are just one minute late for your plane departure? One makes a difference.

- The axis of the planet Earth is tilted at 23.45 degrees. A change of just one degree would be enough to flood large sections of the globe. One makes a difference.

- One apple seed properly planted and cared for can lead to an orchard of apple trees and thousands of apples, with multiple thousands of seeds. One spark in the wrong place can wipe out thousands of trees. One makes a difference.

- In 1923, one single vote gave one man the leadership role of his political party. It was the Nazi Party, and the man was Adolf Hitler. One makes a difference.

- For every historical event of significance there was one single person who made a difference (e.g., Abraham, Moses, Jesus, Martin Luther, Christopher Columbus, George Washington, Abraham Lincoln, and every mother!). One makes a difference.

- You are one person, and each person with whom you share the gift can make a profound difference, with a possibility of making a difference for hundreds and thousands of others. One makes a difference.

If you learn and live these priceless principles, you will be empowered and propelled into your better future, and you will be able to live life fully and find your treasure. Remember, not only is your future at stake, but people's very lives are at stake. And when you win, lots of others win, too! Who you are and what you do make a difference!

Chapter 10
Raise Your Self Esteem for Success in Network Marketing

Emotions are all around us in the office, and it's important for leaders to understand how to harness them to cultivate productivity and positive relationships. Learn what emotional intelligence is and how it factors in at work and discover concrete techniques for raising your own emotional quotient (EQ). This includes perceiving yourself accurately, exercising emotional self-control, practicing resilience, and developing empathy. Then turn those lessons around to build your awareness of others and learn to inspire helpful communication and manage conflict.

When it comes to your self-worth, only one opinion truly matters — your own. And even that one should be carefully evaluated; we tend to be our own harshest critics.

"Unconditional human worth assumes that each of us is born with all the capacities needed to live fruitfully, although everyone has a different mix of skills, which are at different levels of development." He emphasizes that core worth is independent of externals that the marketplace values, such as wealth, education, health, status — or the way one has been treated.

Some navigate the world — and relationships — searching for any bit of evidence to validate their self-limiting beliefs. Much like judge and jury, they constantly put themselves on trial and sometimes sentence themselves to a lifetime of self-criticism.

Following are eight steps you can take to increase your feelings of self-worth.

1. Be mindful.
We can't change something if we don't recognize that there is something to change. By simply becoming aware of our negative self-talk, we begin to distance ourselves from the feelings it brings up. This enables us to identify with them less. Without this awareness, we can easily fall into the trap of believing our self-limiting talk, and "Don't believe everything you think. Thoughts are just that — thoughts."

As soon as you find yourself going down the path of self-criticism, gently note what is happening, be curious about it, and remind yourself, "These are thoughts, not facts."

2. Change the story.
We all have a narrative or a story we've created about ourselves that shapes our self-perceptions, upon which our core self-image is based. If we want to change that story, we have to understand where it came from and where we received the messages we tell ourselves. Whose voices are we internalizing?
"Sometimes automatic negative thoughts like 'you're fat' or 'you're lazy' can be repeated in your mind so often that you start to believe they are true," These thoughts are learned, which means they can be unlearned. You can start with affirmations. What do you wish you believed about yourself? Repeat these phrases to yourself every day."

3. Avoid falling into the compare-and-despair rabbit hole.
"Two key things emphasize in are to practice acceptance and stop comparing yourself to others," emphasis that just because someone else appears happy on social media or even in person doesn't mean they are happy. Comparisons only lead to negative self-talk, which leads to anxiety and stress." Feelings of low self-worth can negatively affect your mental health as well as other areas in your life, such as work, relationships, and physical health.

4. Channel your inner rock star.
Everybody is a genius. But if you judge a fish by its ability to climb a tree, it will live its whole life believing that it is stupid." We all have our strengths and weaknesses. Someone may be a brilliant musician, but a dreadful cook. Neither quality defines their core worth. Recognize what your strengths are and the feelings of confidence they engender, especially in times of doubt. It's easy to make generalizations when you "mess up" or "fail" at something, but reminding yourself of the ways you rock offers a more realistic perspective of yourself.
 "Was there a time in your life where you had better self-esteem? What were you doing at that stage of your life?" If it's difficult for you to identify your unique gifts, ask a friend to point them out to you. Sometimes it's easier for others to see the best in us than it is for us to see it in ourselves.

5. Exercise.

Many studies have shown a correlation between exercise and higher self-esteem, as well as improved mental health. "Exercising creates empowerment both physical and mental," especially weight lifting where you can calibrate the accomplishments. Exercise organizes your day around self-care." She suggests dropping a task daily from your endless to-do list for the sole purpose of relaxation or doing something fun, and seeing how that feels. Other forms of self-care, such as proper nutrition and sufficient sleep, have also been shown to have positive effects on one's self-perception.

6. Do unto others.

To help those who may be less fortunate. "Being of service to others helps take you out of your head. When you are able to help someone else, it makes you less focused on your own issues."

"What I find is that the more someone does something in their life that they can be proud of, the easier it is for them to recognize their worth. Doing things that one can respect about them is the one key that I have found that works to raise one's worth. It is something tangible. Helping at a homeless shelter, animal shelter, giving of time at a big brother or sister organization. These are things that mean something and give value to not only oneself, but to someone else as well."

There is much truth to the fact that what we put out there into the world tends to boomerang back to us. To test this out, spend a day intentionally putting out positive thoughts and behaviors toward those with whom you come into contact. As you go about your day, be mindful of what comes back to you, and also notice if your mood improves.

7. Forgiveness.

Is there is someone in your life you haven't forgiven? An ex-partner? A family member? Yourself? By holding on to feelings of bitterness or resentment, we keep ourselves stuck in a cycle of negativity. If we haven't forgiven ourselves, shame will keep us in this same loop.

"Forgiving self and others have been found to improve self-esteem," "Perhaps because it connects us with our innately loving nature and promotes an acceptance of people, despite our flaws." He refers to the Buddhist meditation on forgiveness, which can be practiced at any time: "If I have hurt or harmed anyone, knowingly or unknowingly, I ask forgiveness. If anyone has hurt or harmed me, knowingly or unknowingly,

I forgive them. For the ways I have hurt myself, knowingly or unknowingly, I offer forgiveness."

8. Remember that you are not your circumstances.
Finally, learning to differentiate between your circumstances and who you are is key to self-worth. "Recognizing inner worth, and loving one's imperfect self, provides the secure foundation for growth," "With that security, one is free to grow with enjoyment, not fear of failure — because failure doesn't change core worth."

We are all born with infinite potential and equal worth as human beings. That we are anything less is a false belief that we have learned over time. Therefore, with hard work and self-compassion, self-destructive thoughts and beliefs can be unlearned. Taking the steps outlined above is a start in the effort to increase self-worth, "recognize self-worth. It already exists in each person."

CREATE A VISION FOR YOUR LIFE THAT HONORS YOU'RE MOST IMPORTANT VALUES

Our minds cannot tell the difference between actual reality and experiences that are vividly imagined. This is the reason that we laugh, cry, or scream at funny, sad, or scary movies. We get what we clearly envision and expect. We can take advantage of this ability to tap into what we want and expect to experience through our network marketing businesses by creating a vivid, written vision that inspires and empowers us and others to do what it takes to realize the vision.

I invite you to give up your right to invalidate yourself by keeping any of your negative expectations in place. Instead, create a vision that is filled with positive expectations for what your life will be like as a result of your network marketing success. This vision must honor your most important values.
Perhaps these might include any of the following: freedom, adventure, belonging, creativity, contribution, love, excitement, happiness, peace, joy, recognition, security, and inspiration, just to name a few.

Include in your vision the answers to these questions:

1) What will you be known for, what qualities will you embody, and what values will you honor as you live your life and work your business?

2) What sort of activities will you typically do? What will a customary day at work look like? How will you spend your free time? What passions and hobbies will you pursue?

3) What will you have as a result of who you are being and because of your successful efforts? Where will you live and with whom? Describe in detail your house, cars, and all toys and material possessions with which you'll surround yourself.

4) Who are the people and special causes to which you'll contribute? How will you impact the lives of your family, friends, and network marketing partners? Remember, any vision that is about only you will not inspire others to join you in its accomplishment or inspire them to create visions of their own.

5) Picture yourself building your business successfully. What will your organization look like? How will others see you? For what accomplishments will you be recognized? Picture yourself interacting with others in a way that reflects your high self-esteem and the rich relationships you have established.

Write out your vision in the first person, present tense to describe every aspect of your life and business. Say, "I am experiencing material abundance and rich, rewarding friendships" rather than "I will experience" or "I hope to experience." Remember, we get what we expect. So, if you expect that you will (but are not now) experiencing or hope to achieve (but are not now achieving), your mind will manifest a reality consistent with these images of lacking what you want.

Read your vision at least twice daily. After doing so for at least 30 days, your subconscious will begin to create a physical and mental state consistent with what is needed to manifest your vision.

CREATE AN ACTION PLAN CONSISTENT WITH YOUR VISION
Network marketing has the potential to provide each of us with the level of income that can free us up to pursue our passions and honor our most

critical values. Ask yourself, how much income it will take for me to realize all aspects of my vision? Who will I need to be and what will I need to do to make my vision come to pass?

Determine how many leaders you will need to develop and duplicate to achieve the income level you desire. From there, determine what your success ratios are: how many prospects will you need to speak with in order to identify and develop this many leaders? For example, if you know that you'll typically need to speak with 100 prospects to identify one do-whatever-it-takes leader, and your goal is to identify one new leader each month, you may need to speak with five prospects daily, five days per week in order to hit your desired number. As part of your plan, you'll also need to determine where and how you'll find your prospects, what you'll say and give them, and to whom and how you'll introduce them as a next step. For a more detailed explanation involving all aspects of how to create an effective action plan, see my book, the 7-Step System to Building a $1,000,000 Network Marketing Dynasty.

MANAGE NEGATIVE SELF-TALK AND ACT FROM YOUR NEWLY INVENTED
DECLARATION OF WHO YOU ARE

We all experience that nasty, negative, doubting the voice of our negative self-talker whispering in our ear from time to time. The trouble begins when we forget that the voice is not speaking the truth and buy into those lies. This negative self-talk serves only to keep us from risking, preferring that we play small instead, in an effort to protect us from harm—otherwise known as rejection and what we interpret as a failure. I suggest that you decide today to live by two new rules designed to support your belief in yourself and in your ultimate success as a network marketing leader. They are:

1. Give up your right to invalidate yourself or buy into any negative opinions you or others may have about you.

2. Decide today to act from a declaration of who you say you are. No evidence for this new, empowering declaration is required. In fact, you'll now be creating new positive evidence as you go.

Take all of the qualities you have decided to manifest in your life and business and craft a new declaration that speaks to who you are now deciding to be a powerful leader. Use this as a statement from which to live. State your empowered declaration, like your vision, in the first person, a present positive minded leader committed to contributing to the lives of all I touch. I powerfully share the gift of my networking opportunity with a positive belief in its value to impact others' lives as well as my own."

Whenever you notice that you have fallen back into any old habits of questioning your ability or doubting your future success, simply remind yourself that this is not who you are. Give yourself a break; decide again to believe in yourself and step into a confident posture that will support your business success.

AFFIRM YOUR STRENGTHS AND ACKNOWLEDGE YOURSELF DAILY

We all have strengths and gifts that make us uniquely special and magnificent in our own ways. At times, we all temporarily lose belief in ourselves and in our ability to succeed in our businesses by impacting others' lives with our products and opportunity. We forget to focus on the awesome gift we can be in providing our opportunity to others and instead pay too much attention to our own fears and petty concerns. We become adept at recognizing all our weaknesses and identifying all the reasons why we fear we will not be successful in our quest to realize our dreams.

Instead of focusing on these challenges, get into the habit of recognizing the little things you do well. Catch yourself doing something right and acknowledge yourself for it. Ask yourself, "What did I do well today? What can I commend myself for this morning?" By looking for excuses to pat yourself on the back, you'll start to become more aware of all the things for which you really should be commended. Write yourself a daily brief paragraph outlining these worthy attributes and accomplishments. This can be as simple as congratulating yourself for speaking to a prospect that you may not have ordinarily approached or asking questions to get to know someone better and build rapport.

Our conscious minds can entertain only one thought at a time. As the gatekeepers to our minds, it's up to us whether we allow that present thought to be a negative, fearful, or disempowering one, or a positive, affirming belief instead. We have the ability to manage our thoughts moment by moment. The more we get into the habit of substituting positive instead of negative thoughts, the easier this process will become.

Write out a series of positive affirmations that speak directly to any negative or disempowering beliefs that would influence your network marketing outcome. Again, write your affirmations out in first person, present tense.

Write such statements as:

- I am a powerful enroller, able to contribute the gift of personal and financial freedom to others.

- I am a good listener, aware of what's important to others and missing in their lives.

- People like me, trust me, and want to learn about the benefits I share.

- I make friends easily.

- I act consistently and persistently, performing the massive action required bringing about my great success.

- I inspire others to make their lives work optimally because of my courage in sharing our opportunity.

Keep these affirmations by your phone, on your nightstand, on your mirror, in your car, and everywhere else to remind you of your power as you go about your day.

TAKE ON A PERSONAL DEVELOPMENT PROGRAM
One of the best ways I know to take the rejection out of building a network marketing business while adding fun and fulfillment is to create a structure to develop those personal and leadership qualities you see as enhancing your life and business.

This can be as simple as selecting a quality to work on in your prospecting conversations and then rating yourself (1 to 10) as to how well you did after each conversation. When I began my business, due to excessive nervousness and a fear of being judged and rejected, I had a tendency to dump too much information on my prospects. I soon realized that just sharing a lot of details about my company, products, and income opportunity was not very effective in motivating them to join our team. Instead, I decided to work on the qualities of developing rapport, listening to what was important to my prospects or missing in their lives and creating rich value for them in days before adding another area. Eventually these intentions became habits and my enrollment success numbers shot up dramatically.

Another means of identifying what might be missing from your conversations to make them more effective is by taping your calls. Using an inexpensive cassette recorder and phone device, you can easily record your conversations. By listening to these later, you will often discover areas to improve upon to make your conversations more powerful. You can also ask your success-line partners to listen and give you suggestions regarding how to improve your calls.

CHAMPION YOUR TEAM

Our network marketing businesses not only provide us with an exciting opportunity to reinvent who we are as a possibility for achieving happy, fulfilling lives for ourselves but also offer us the chance to give this same gift to our partners. Our financial success in this business will be directly related to how effective we have been in championing our business partners (downline) to step into their self-confident personal power as they go about their business building activities and support their leaders to do the same.

After experiencing 14 dynamic, life-changing years in the network marketing profession, transforming myself from a shy dentist who "couldn't lead three people in silent prayer" to a self-declared leader with a vision to impact the lives of 20 million people, I am convinced that anyone with a sincere desire can take on a courageous personal reinvention program to support their happiness, personal power, and success. Our networking businesses will grow in direct proportion to both our personal growth (as we increase our attractiveness as a business partner to others) and the level of massive, consistent action we engage in as we build our teams. As we take on more confidence and strengthen our belief in our ability to impact others' lives with our income opportunity, our prospects will become more attracted to us as they recognize our confident ability to support them in attaining their dreams.

Conclusion

Network marketing is present everywhere, not just in companies. Teenager boasts the latest video game to classmates and to friends. Visitor's cinemas spread the word about good films and, consequently, you are seeing significantly more viewers than you would otherwise. Best of all this is that such advertising does not cost anything is convincing (about the product we hear from people they know and trust them) and efficient-companies are saving on marketing, advertising.

Part of the savings the company than split between users who are in the first place most deserving of it. In addition, they also offer bonuses if you bring new customers in order to encourage them to potential new customers are actively seeking among their acquaintances. Here then occur companies whose business models are based on this fact. The most famous example of this is Amway.

But it is true, network marketing is sometimes still considered as a pyramid scheme in people's thoughts. And that is because they do not know what it is about. It is a stereotype. I definitely think that network marketing is a good idea if the implementation is right and on the level. And once if you want to succeed, you have to be focused and take time.

I am a distributor for NWorld Company and I have already had experiences with selling. In the beginning, it was not easy at all, but once when people starting to trust you, you are in. Then you can be successful.

--I hope you enjoy reading this book. I would appreciate it if you can leave a feedback in Amazon site.—

With love,

Florino